When Heaven Meets Earth

A 12-Part Biblical Study on Heaven from The Bible Project

Date .... **Session 1** .... **Session 7**
.... **Session 2** .... **Session 8**
.... **Session 3** .... **Session 9**
.... **Session 4** .... **Session 10**
.... **Session 5** .... **Session 11**
.... **Session 6** .... **Session 12**

Completed by ....

Printed in China
ISBN 978 0 9984168 1 6

Written by Timothy Mackie & Jonathan Collins

Art Direction by Robert Perez
Illustrations by Mac Cooper & Shiela Laufer
Layout Design by Xela Gold

Editing by
Melissa Binder (Developmental and Line Editor)
Whitney Woollard (Copy Editor)
Sherry Hames (Proofreader)

Scripture quotations without any marking are our own translations from the original language.

thebibleproject.com

| Table of Contents

How to Use This Guide

This study guide consists of 12 sessions that you can tackle alone or with a group. Either way, we recommend undertaking only one session at a time, as each comes with a hefty load of recommended Scripture reading. If you're leading a group, visit our website to download tips for guiding the study.

Our URL is thebibleproject.com

We'll be moving through the biblical narrative chronologically, from the Garden of Eden to the construction of Solomon's temple to John's visions about the realization of a new creation. Each session begins with selections from biblical texts that we believe best set the stage for the lesson, but we'll also point diligent readers to other passages for deeper context.

You'll find recommended readings over here in the margin, which we also use for providing helpful tips, like this one.

Each session follows a consistent structure. We start with a lesson that captures the essential ideas of the session. Then, we move on to "Geek Out," where we dig into the nerdy weeds of one or two concepts. Next up is "Dig Deeper," where we invite you to examine relevant biblical stories like a true scholar—but with a little guidance. We'll wrap up with a handful of discussion questions. If you're working through this book alone, consider these questions as prompts for journaling.

It's important to note that we use a few different modern translations for most of the quoted and referenced Scripture passages: the New Revised Standard Version (NRSV), the New International Version (NIV), and the English Standard Version (ESV). If a Scripture quotation is not cited, that means Tim Mackie provided the translation, usually to highlight a specific word from the original language. If you have a different translation at home, be aware that the study might focus on the importance of a word that you don't see in your particular English version.

Feel free to use the blank margin space for note-taking. That's why it's here.

Let's begin!

Big Picture

Imagine heaven.

See clouds? A pearly gate? Golden walls? For most of us, the word "heaven" conjures up a cartoonish image of a city floating on cotton, even if that's not really what we believe God's dwelling place is like. Time to forget all that.

In this study, we want you to begin to think about heaven the way the Bible thinks about heaven.

This 5-minute animated video is an introduction to the ideas that we explore in this workbook. It is a perfect way to begin your exploration into the biblical theme of Heaven and Earth.

Watch the video at **go.jointhebibleproject.com/heaven+earth**

The Story of Two Domains

The Bible is massive. It's daunting. And the idea of reading it all in order—well, that sounds like a New Year's resolution we've all tried and failed.

But we believe the Bible is a profound and beautiful book telling one complete story from beginning to end, and we believe that one of the main themes of that story is the relationship between heaven and earth.

When we use the words "heaven" and "earth," we are talking about two different domains. Heaven is God's domain. It is ruled by God. In heaven, God is the one who defines what is good and what is evil. It's where God's will is always done. The biblical authors call this domain by different names, including God's kingdom, paradise, eternal life, and, of course, heaven.

Earth is our domain. On earth, humans have chosen to be the ones who define good and evil. Biblical authors give this domain a few different names, too: the world, the present age, and the age of sin and death. Notice that two of those names imply that humanity's domain is only temporary, an age, which, by definition, comes to an end.

The story of the Bible is the story of heaven *on* earth being ripped into heaven *and* earth, followed by God's glorious mission to reunite these two realms once again.

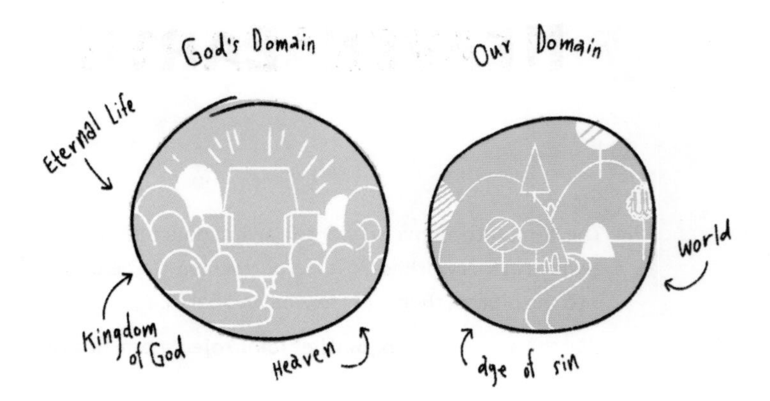

The 30,000-Foot View

The Bible opens with God's domain and humanity's domain completely overlapping. It was literally heaven on earth—God's domain flourishing on our beloved ball of rock and water. In the Bible, this paradise is represented as the Garden of Eden. But quickly we come to a rift. Humans rebelled, deciding they wanted a domain where they could define good and evil on their own terms.

From Genesis 3 onward, the basic tension driving the story of the Bible is how God is going to rejoin heaven and earth. And that's ultimately where the story ends: with a vision, a promise of divine space and human space united once and for all.

So where are we now? According to the biblical narrative, we live in a time when heaven and earth are still disconnected, but not completely. The Bible shows us over and over that these two domains overlap. There are pockets of heaven on earth right now, and they're growing.

This workbook is designed as a thorough investigation of how the Bible discusses the tragic rift, the surprising overlap, and the final uniting of God's domain with our domain.

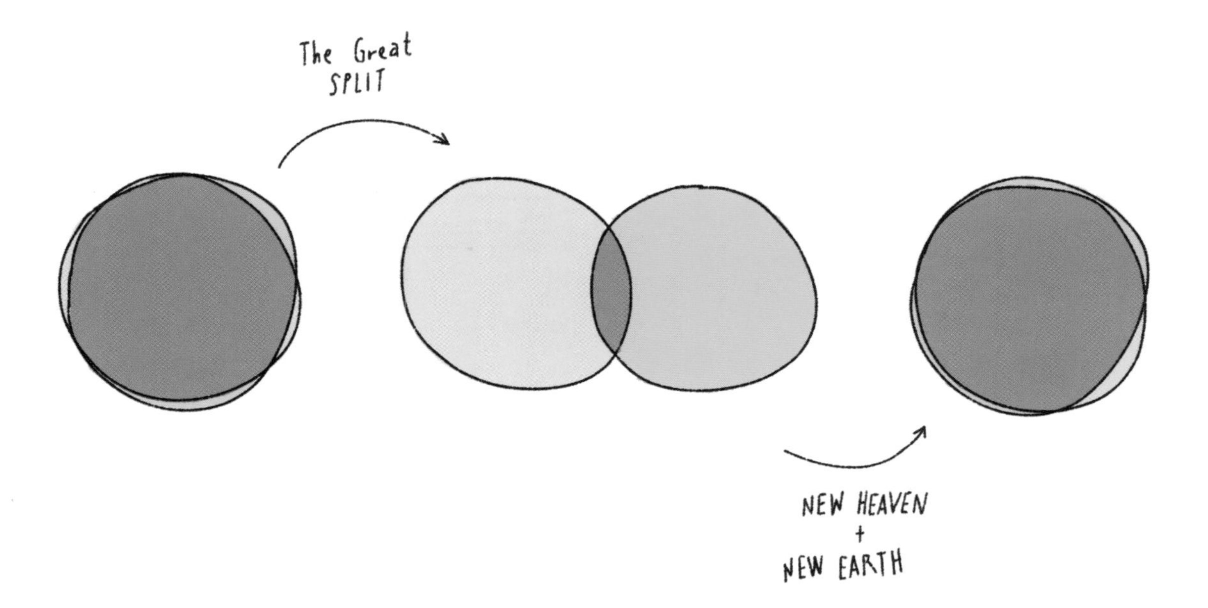

Session 1 | The Heavens as "The Skies"

In the beginning God created the heavens and the earth.

Genesis 1:1 (NIV)

What Are "the Heavens"?

"In the beginning God created the heavens and the earth." The famous opening line of the Bible introduces God as the artist behind everything we know and love in this world. It tells us that from day one God split creation into two categories: heaven and earth. It is pretty clear what earth is. But what should you picture here when you think of heaven?

The word heaven can have many different meanings in English. When most people say "heaven," they are referring to the mystical, spiritual city where some believe they'll go after they die. In modern English, we also use "heaven" as a synonym for "paradise" or "bliss." We casually call our vacation destinations or gourmet desserts "heavenly."

But Genesis 1:1 isn't talking about either of those things when it uses the word "heaven." Instead, the word "heaven" here literally means "the sky."

We need to introduce you to the Hebrew word that we translate as "heavens." The word is pronounced *shamayim*, and it can be translated as the English word "heaven." But there's another, more basic English word that gets at the essence of *shamayim*, namely, "the skies." Sometimes this word is used to refer to the domain in which God dwells and rules (heaven). Other times the word simply means the sky above us. It depends on the context.

The Hebrew word for "the earth" in Genesis 1:1 is *ehrets*. In modern English, we usually use the word "earth" to talk about the whole planet, but *ehrets* means "land," as in the ground we stand on.

In Genesis 1:1, the word *shamayim* is referring to the sky, not to a special domain where God lives. Read the familiar words again, and you'll immediately see that Genesis 1:1 could just as accurately be translated as, "In the beginning God created the skies and the land." The realm where humans live is "the land," and the realm above is "the sky." As the story goes on, each realm is treated separately so that even animals are divided up as either sky animals or land animals.

This might feel underwhelming. Maybe you thought Genesis 1:1 was about God creating the entire universe, the terrestrial ball we call earth, and the supernatural place we call heaven. That sounds exciting. But God making the plain old sky and land? I guess that's cool, but it doesn't seem as exciting as God making an otherworldly place where angels live. After all, apps on our phones tell us what to expect from the sky every day. We can fly through the sky in giant aluminum tubes with wings. We can even get Wi-Fi up there.

To ancient readers, however, the sky was enchanting. It was a realm beyond human reach. They could admire the sky, but not experience it. They depended on it for water and sunlight, but could not fathom its reality. From this perspective, God separating heaven and earth meant separating the domain that humans live in and can learn to control, from the realm that we can see but is beyond our grasp.

In Genesis 1, God isn't creating a supernatural place where he lives separate from human. In fact, the next chapter of Genesis tells us exactly where God lives, and it's not in heaven (spoiler, it's on earth).

The Sky as a Metaphor for God's Domain

In Hebrew, the word for "clouds" is pronounced *shehaqim*. Depending on the context, this word can also be translated as "heaven" or "heavens," though it is much less common than *shamayim*.

Put yourself in the shoes of an ancient Israelite. When you look up into the sky, you are overwhelmed with its beauty and majesty. The skies are one of the most mysterious and awe-inspiring things to behold. The skies are vast and powerful. They are literally above us, as in a position of authority, and we depend on them for life. You can begin to see why the word "sky" became the same word to describe God's domain, heaven. The skies are a perfect metaphor for the glory and transcendence of the domain where God reigns and dwells.

Because of these parallels, the biblical authors almost always used the word for "the skies" to talk about the place where God dwells, but this linguistic tool doesn't necessarily mean they thought God actually lived in the sky (we know their perspective was much more nuanced than that, and we'll explore it more in session 7). Using the same word to mean both "the skies" and "heaven" is more a claim about God's status and authority than it is speculation about the physical location of his presence. To say God lives in heaven means that God shares the same characteristics as the skies. Or, to put it a different way:

> *The Lord is high above all the nations,*
> *and his glory above the heavens.*
> *Who is like the Lord our God,*
> *who is seated on high.*
>
> Psalm 113:4–5 (NRSV)

Why Are "the Heavens" Plural?

In Hebrew, plural nouns are indicated by attaching "*-im*" or "*-ot*" to the end of a word (like "*-s*" in English).

The words "heaven" and "sky" are almost always singular in modern English, but in biblical Hebrew, the word *shamayim* is plural. That's why we sometimes see "skies" or "heavens" in our English Bibles instead of "sky" or "heaven."

Hebrew grammarians call this a "plural of extension," meaning the word is plural because it describes something large or complex. It's a linguistic trick that works well in English, too. By nature, the word "skies" connotes something grander than "sky." It makes sense to think of the realm above us as a vastness of things, not as a single thing. "The sky" doesn't do justice to a clear view of a starry night outside city lights.

WATERS ABOVE
DAY 1
LIGHT
VAULT
DAY 4
SKY STUFF
SKIES
DAY 2
SEPARATE WATERS
DAY 6
LAND CREATURES + HUMANS
DAY 3
SEPARATE LAND + SEA
DAY 5
SKY + SEA CREATURES
LAND
SEA
SHEOL
DAY 7
REST
WATERS BELOW

Geek Out

The Three-Tiered View of the Universe (Biblical Cosmology)

Today, we understand that the earth is a planet spinning around a star in one small section of a vast network of galaxies. However, biblical authors had a much different view of the cosmos than we do. (After all, they didn't have telescopes.)

The ancient Israelites and their neighbors understood the universe as three realms stacked on top of one another, which scholars of ancient Near Eastern history describe as three tiers:

TIER 1: THE WATERS BELOW
As far as ancient people could tell, their land was surrounded by water on every side. They also knew you'd hit water if you dug deep enough. They imagined all this water was connected as one vast sea all around and underneath. And for them, the sea represented chaos and was perceived as dangerous and impossible to rule.

The land is kept from sinking into the waters below by the "pillars of the earth" (see Psalm 75:3 or 1 Samuel 2:8), and its flat disc-shape is called "the circle of the earth" (see Isaiah 40:22).

TIER 2: THE LAND
Because they perceived all the water to be connected, they imagined land as a kind of disc that was floating in the great sea. They believed all human life existed on this one disc.

TIER 3: THE SKIES
Ancient people imagined that there was a giant dome over the land and sea, like the glass of a snow globe. They believed there was water above this dome, and that rain was water leaking through the dome. They saw the sun, moon and stars as embedded into the dome itself.

The Hebrew word for the dome is *raqia*. It appears for the first time in Genesis 1:6, and is best translated as "dome" or "vault," the latter of which captures the dome's supposed role of holding back waters high above. When it rains, the water above the dome are being released through "windows" (see Genesis 7:11)

You can see the three-tiered view of the universe woven into Genesis 1:

DAY 0 GENESIS 1:2 God's Spirit hovers over the chaotic and unordered state of the cosmos before God brings order and beauty to it.

DAY 1 GENESIS 1:3-5 God creates light and separates it from darkness. Here "light" is not the energy that emanates from the sun or is reflected off the moon. God calls the light "day," which is a period of time, not a physical entity. God departing light and dark, day and night, is an ancient Israelite way of saying that God created the fixed order of time itself.

DAY 2 GENESIS 1:6-8 God separates the waters above from the waters below by means of the dome, which holds back the waters above. He calls the dome the "sky."

DAY 3 GENESIS 1:9-13 God separates the land from the sea, and then summons the land to generate vegetation.

DAY 4 GENESIS 1:14-19 God places the sun, moon, and stars in the dome and appoints them as markers for the passage of time.

DAY 5 GENESIS 1:20-23 God creates the creatures that live in the sea and the creatures that live in the sky.

DAY 6 GENESIS 1:24-31 God summons the land to generate creatures, and, finally, he appoints humans in his image to rule the land on his behalf.

DAY 7 GENESIS 2:1-3 God rests.

Dig Deeper

In the Old Testament, the English words "heaven" or "heavens" are almost always a translation of the Hebrew word *shamayim*, which you now know means "skies." But when the authors wrote *shamayim*, they weren't always trying to talk about God's domain or dwelling place. In most cases, they were simply referring to the atmosphere. Let's practice learning to tell the difference by looking at the context of some biblical texts.

1.

Look up the following verses and notice that the use of the word "heaven" simply refers to the sky. (Remember, whether the word is singular or plural depends on your translation, but in Hebrew, it's always plural).

a. **Genesis 7:19**
b. **Deuteronomy 4:11**
c. **Psalm 8:3**

2.

In other contexts, "the skies" can refer to God's dwelling place. For instance, Psalm 11:4 says "his throne is in the skies." Here, the authors are using the sky as a metaphor to refer to God's transcendent authority over all things. Turn to the following verses and observe how "heavens" is being used as a metaphor for God's royal domain.

a. **Psalm 14:2**
b. **Psalm 33:13–14**
c. **Psalm 102:19**
d. **Psalm 103:19**

Discussion

What images come to mind when you think about heaven?
Where do those ideas come from, and what emotions do they conjure up?

Describe the feelings and thoughts you have when you admire the sky.
Discuss the quality of the sky and how it is different from land.

What metaphors or descriptions besides the sky are used today to talk about God's location?

Notes

Session 2 | The Garden Temple

And the Lord God planted a garden in Eden, in the east; and there he put the man whom he had formed. Out of the ground the Lord God made to grow every tree that is pleasant to the sight and good for food…

Genesis 2:8–9 (NRSV)

Then the man and his wife heard the sound of the Lord God as he was walking in the garden in the cool of the day…

Genesis 3:8a (NIV)

The Grand Garden

Now that we've established an understanding of the skies and their role as a metaphor for God's domain, it's time to zoom in on the land.

In Genesis 2, we find that God created a garden where humans work and explore and create with God. In the Bible, this space is called the Garden of Eden, a bountiful and sacred home.

The Hebrew word *eden* is used elsewhere in the Bible to mean "bliss" or "delight." For example, the phrase "the river of delights" in Psalm 36:9 is literally "the river of eden." An alternative translation of "Garden of Eden" would be "garden of delight."

The Garden of Eden is described as an amazing place. Don't picture your grandma's garden or even your local botanical garden. Ancient gardens were impressive, massive spaces created by kings as oases of life. Here is a description of a garden in Nineveh created by an Assyrian king named Ashurnasirpal II who lived between 883–859 B.C.:

> "I dug out a canal from the (river) Upper Zab, cutting through a mountain peak, and called it the Abundance Canal. I watered the meadows of the Tigris and planted orchards with all kinds of fruit trees in the vicinity. I planted seeds and plants that I had found in the countries through which I had marched and in the highlands which I had crossed: pines of different kinds, cypresses and junipers of different kinds, almonds, dates, ebony, rosewood, olive, oak, tamarisk, walnut, terebinth and ash, fir, pomegranate, pear, quince, fig, grapevine.... The canal water gushes from above into the garden; fragrance pervades the walkways, streams of water as numerous as the stars of heaven flow in the pleasure garden… Like a squirrel I pick fruit in the garden of delights…"[1]

The Garden of Eden wasn't designed by a human king, of course, so we can imagine it was even grander. And unlike other ancient gardens, the Garden of Eden was not a destination to visit, but a place for humans to live and work in community with God.

1 For more on ancient gardens, check out Stephanie Dalley's *The Mystery of the Hanging Garden of Babylon: An Elusive World Wonder Traced* (Oxford University Press, 2013).

An Introduction to Ancient Temples

In an ancient city, the only site as grand as the king's garden would have been the temple. Ancient temples were designated spaces where humans could experience the presence of the gods. They were arguably the most marvelous structures in the ancient world.

From the ziggurats of ancient Mesopotamia to the pyramids of ancient Egypt to the massive Mayan temples in South America, these buildings were designed to evoke transcendence and awe. Only priests were allowed inside most temples, because they functioned as mediators between the gods and the people of the city. Temples were revered, exclusive spaces, often guarded by soldiers and large statues of animal-like creatures.

The Garden as God's Temple

The Hebrew word for "image" in the phrase "image of God" is pronounced *tselem* (see Genesis 1:27). It's one of the common Hebrew words to refer to idol.

In Genesis 1:26–28, God designates humans as his image, giving them "dominion over the fish of the sea, and over the birds of the air, and over the cattle, and over all the wild animals of the earth, and over every creeping thing that creeps upon the earth."

In order to meet with God you had to go to a temple, which is why the beginning of the biblical story is so fascinating. God didn't create a temple for himself. Instead, he planted a garden where he dwelled with humans.

The garden was his temple. Humans had full access to God, and God had full access to humans. No soldiers or scary statues standing in the way.

We know God saw the garden as his temple not only because he dwelled there, but also because of a key word used in the Genesis narrative: "image." In the inner recesses of every ancient temple, you would find a statue of the god that the temple was built to honor. These statues were considered physical embodiments of the god's presence and authority in the land, and they were called "idols" or "images."

Here's the remarkable thing. In Genesis, God declared that humans were his image. Instead of setting a statue in one specific place in the garden to symbolize his reign, he commissioned the living, breathing humans to be the figures that represented his rule. To be made in the image of God means we have been given God's authority to reign and rule over creation on his behalf. And that is exactly what we see happen next. God ordered humans to multiply and subdue all of creation. God freed humans to use their own creative power and imagination to spread the order and beauty of the garden into the rest of creation.

Genesis 2 gives us a picture of God's domain and humanity's domain completely overlapping. It was heaven on earth—a glorious time when God's space and humans' space were one and the same.

Geek Out

The Significance of Seven Days

The seven-day structure of the creation narrative in Genesis 1:1–2:3 is both confusing and controversial today, but the ancient Israelites would not have fretted over whether the narrative was accurate or metaphorical. Instead, they would have heard another message loud and clear: Creation is God's temple.

In the ancient Israelites' world, temples were always dedicated with a seven-day ceremony. This was true not only of the Israelites' temples built for their God, but of temples among neighboring nations raised for their deities. We have ancient records that describe a seven-day ritual for a temple built by a Sumerian king more than 1,000 years before Solomon erected the great temple of Jerusalem. This ritual was so deeply ingrained in ancient culture that the Israelites would have immediately understood a seven-day creation story to mean that creation itself was a temple for their God.

In the Old Testament, we witness three other seven-day ritual dedications connected to temples.

LEVITICUS 8:33–35
The Israelites held a seven-day ceremony to dedicate the sacred tabernacle in the wilderness.

1 KINGS 8:2 AND 8:65
Solomon dedicates the temple in Jerusalem with two back-to-back seven-day ceremonies in the seventh month of the calendar year.

EZEKIEL 43:25–27
The prophet envisions a new temple in Jerusalem and foresees a seven-day ritual dedication.

Geek Out

The Real Meaning of "Rest"

On the seventh day of creation's dedication ceremony, we're told that God rested and blessed the day to set it apart. But "rest" in this context isn't quite what we imagine as modern English speakers.

The word "rest" in Hebrew, pronounced *shabat*, does not mean "rest" in the sense of "relaxation." The word means, more precisely, "to cease." For example, manna "ceased" to appear on the ground once Israel arrived in the Promised Land, and Job's friends "ceased" arguing with him when they realized he would never see things their way.

On the seventh day, God ceased.

So, what did God do after he ceased the work of creation? Well, for that, we look to another important Hebrew word used to talk about the meaning of the Sabbath and God's rest. The verb is spelled *nuakh*, and the noun variation is *menukhah*. The word means "settling in." It is used to describe how locusts settle upon a field to devour it or how a group of people settle in a land. It's a word that implies new activities are beginning, activities appropriate for a new time or place. For instance, in 2 Samuel 7:1, God instructed David to *nuakh* in Jerusalem, which meant he could take up the work of running his kingdom.

God's Sabbath was not a withdrawal from the world and its operations. It was not a vacation or a nap. Rather, it was the point at which he stopped bringing order to creation and took his place at the helm of what had been created.

After God ceased, he settled in.

The Hebrew word *shabat*, which means "to cease," is the origin of the word and practice of Sabbath in the Jewish and Christian traditions.

Dig Deeper

In the early chapters of Genesis, special care is taken to connect creation to ancient temples. God designates humans as his image on earth, just as ancient worshippers placed a statue of their god in the heart of a temple, and the seven-day structure of creation clearly parallels seven-day dedication ceremonies.

The connection between the garden and Israelite temples doesn't stop there. God instructed Israelite leaders to incorporate garden imagery into the tabernacle and, later, the temple. Let's take a look at how garden symbols and images show up in Israelite structures in order to imitate the atmosphere of Eden.

1.

Grab a highlighter. As you read the following passages, mark every single garden, plant, and precious metal you come across. A sparkling garden will grow right in front of you as you read.

a. **Exodus 25–31** (the tabernacle blueprints)
b. **1 Kings 6–7** (the temple designs)

2.

Reread **Genesis 1 and 2**, and reflect on the similarities between the garden and the buildings you just read about. Consider the effect these spaces had on the Israelites who entered them and why God would have told the Israelites to incorporate garden images into buildings designed to house God's presence among his people.

Draw the garden you've found!

Discussion

Imagine entering an ancient temple.
What thoughts and feelings does the space arouse?
How do those connect to your experience with God?

What thoughts and feelings arise as you stroll through or even work in a garden?
How do those connect to your experience with God?

When have you experienced God's divine presence in nature or in the ordinary work of daily life?

Is your life marked by living in the presence of God in your work and play?

Notes

Session 3 | The Great Split

The Lord God took the man and put him in the Garden of Eden to work it and keep it. And the Lord God commanded the man, saying, "You may surely eat of every tree of the garden, but of the tree of the knowledge of good and evil you shall not eat, for in the day that you eat of it you shall surely die."

Genesis 2:15–17 (ESV)

Now the serpent was more crafty than any of the wild animals the Lord God had made. He said to the woman, "Did God really say, 'You must not eat from any tree in the garden'?"

The woman said to the serpent, "We may eat fruit from the trees in the garden, but God did say, 'You must not eat fruit from the tree that is in the middle of the garden, and you must not touch it, or you will die.'"

"You will not certainly die," the serpent said to the woman. "For God knows that when you eat from it your eyes will be opened, and you will be like God, knowing good and evil."

When the woman saw that the fruit of the tree was good for food and pleasing to the eye, and also desirable for gaining wisdom, she took some and ate it. She also gave some to her husband, who was with her, and he ate it. Then the eyes of both of them were opened, and they realized they were naked; so they sewed fig leaves together and made coverings for themselves.

Then the man and his wife heard the sound of the Lord God as he was walking in the garden in the cool of the day, and they hid from the Lord God among the trees of the garden. But the Lord God called to the man, "Where are you?"

He answered, "I heard you in the garden, and I was afraid because I was naked; so I hid."

And he said, "Who told you that you were naked? Have you eaten from the tree that I commanded you not to eat from?"

The man said, "The woman you put here with me—she gave me some fruit from the tree, and I ate it."

Then the Lord God said to the woman, "What is this you have done?"

The woman said, "The serpent deceived me, and I ate."

Genesis 3:1–13 (NIV)

To Adam he said, "Because you listened to your wife and ate fruit from the tree about which I commanded you, 'You must not eat from it,'

"Cursed is the ground because of you;
through painful toil you will eat food from it
all the days of your life.
It will produce thorns and thistles for you,
and you will eat the plants of the field.
By the sweat of your brow
you will eat your food
until you return to the ground,
since from it you were taken;
for dust you are
and to dust you will return."

Adam named his wife Eve, because she would become the mother of all the living.

The Lord God made garments of skin for Adam and his wife and clothed them. And the Lord God said, "The man has now become like one of us, knowing good and evil. He must not be allowed to reach out his hand and take also from the tree of life and eat, and live forever." So the Lord God banished him from the Garden of Eden to work the ground from which he had been taken. After he drove the man out, he placed on the east side of the Garden of Eden cherubim and a flaming sword flashing back and forth to guard the way to the tree of life.

Genesis 3:17–24 (NIV)

The Great Split

Genesis 3 is a strange story. Talking snakes? A magical tree? This text has puzzled and intrigued readers for thousands of years.

There's so much to stop and explore here, but remember, we're focused on a much bigger story—a cosmic story about two overlapping domains that split apart and, with time and sacrifice, are slowly being united again.

Genesis 3 is the story of that split—how our space became separated from God's space, how heaven *on* earth became heaven *and* earth.

At the heart of the tear is humanity's decision to define good and evil for itself. And, as a result, it was banished to the east, no longer allowed open access to God.

Banishment to the east is not random. East of ancient Israel was a huge desert that stretches all the way to ancient Assyria and Babylon. Much later, Israel was banished to trek through that desert again after their centuries-long failure to keep their covenant with God.

We've seen that living inside the garden resulted in abundant life, abundant food, freedom, and the opportunity to partner with God in expanding creation. In Genesis 3, we learn what's outside the garden: toil, frustration, and, ultimately, death. Inside the garden, humans had full access to God. Outside the garden, large animal-like creatures block entry to his holy presence.

The Tree of the Knowledge of Good and Evil

The cause of the split centers around a tree called "the tree of the knowledge of good and evil." Adam and Eve are told not to eat of it or they will die. That's pretty ominous. But, to modern readers, the name "the tree of the knowledge of good and evil" doesn't sound too bad. Knowledge is good, right? Isn't an understanding of morality something we strive for?

The tree of the knowledge of good and evil has historically been depicted as an apple tree, but the Hebrew text does not specify what kind of tree it was.

But let's look at the context of the words "good and evil" to see how we should think about this tree. Up to this point in the biblical story, God has been defining what was good. He does it over and over in Genesis 1. It should be clear to us that God alone has the wisdom and authority to define what is good (and by extension, what is evil). God was warning them against improperly seizing this authority. Do not eat the tree of the knowledge of good and evil.

In Genesis 1, God calls the world he created "good" seven times. In each case, this pronouncement happens after God creates something that will be beneficial for human flourishing. In this way, the author makes it clear that God is the provider and definer of all that is "good."

The story makes it very clear that while humans had a lot of freedom and authority to rule over God's creation, they were not God. They were like God because they were made in the divine image. But they didn't get to be God, which meant they didn't get to define good and evil for themselves. They needed to trust God's wisdom about good and evil.

But along came a serpent, a mysterious figure whose purpose is to deceive. It suggests that seizing this knowledge will make them "like God." He didn't just present them with an opportunity to try a tasty snack. He presented them with an opportunity to usurp God's moral authority.

The basic meaning of this tree is that it represented a choice. Would the humans trust God's knowledge and definition of good and evil, or would they seize the opportunity to know and therefore define good and evil for themselves?

Humans chose autonomy, prioritizing knowledge of good and evil above knowledge of God. By deciding to define good and evil for themselves, Adam and Eve essentially fashioned crude crowns for themselves and declared themselves rulers. They rejected their blessed role as images of God, and instead claimed to be gods.

It was this decision that caused heaven and earth to split apart.

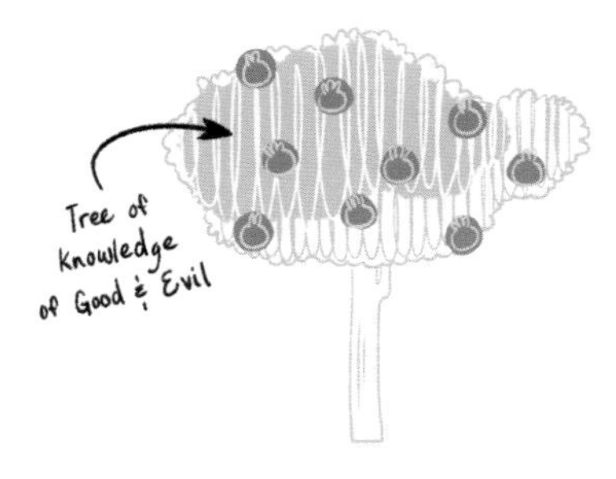

Geek Out

The Tree of Life

The lead tree in this story is undoubtedly the tree of the knowledge of good and evil. That's the tree everyone remembers. But there was a second symbolic tree in the garden of Eden: the tree of life.

Fun fact: Once Gilgamesh finally found the plant, it was stolen by a serpent.

The tree of life was a popular motif in the literature of Israel's neighbors. The famous Babylonian epic of Gilgamesh involves a hunt for a magic plant that bestows youth and perpetual vitality, and ancient Egyptian literature refers to a sycamore that's considered life-giving. Archaeologists have even discovered old depictions of such a tree, like this potsherd fragment found in the borderlands between Egypt and Israel. It dates to the ninth century B.C. and is one of our earliest depictions of the tree of life.

The tree of life is a strategic prop in the biblical story. It's hardly mentioned, but its presence is significant. First, the tree of life is referenced as standing in the center of the Garden of Eden. Then, at the very end of the biblical narrative, it's mentioned again in John's vision of the renewed creation: "On either side of the river is the tree of life with its twelve kinds of fruit, producing its fruit each month; and the leaves of the tree are for the healing of the nations." (Revelation 22:2 NASB)

The tree of life also gets a nod in Proverbs 3:18, 11:30, 13:12, and 15:4, where wisdom is described as a life-giving tree that restores divine blessing.

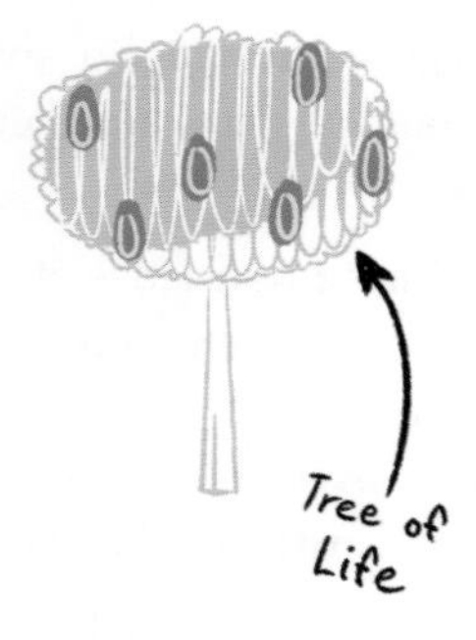

It's important to note that Genesis 3 does not suggest the tree of life has magical powers to bestow life independently. The Bible is very clear that God is the giver of life. In the garden, the tree of life symbolizes the reality that being in close proximity to God's presence is life itself. To live near the author and source of all life is to live forever. To get that point across, the author of Genesis adapted a symbol familiar to his Israelite readers.

Geek Out

Cherubim and Swords

After Adam and Eve exited the garden, Genesis 3 tells us God placed cherubim and a flaming sword at the entrance to guard the way to the tree of life.

What in the world?

First, let's be clear about something, cherubim are not pudgy babies with wings. Cherubim were intimidating, other-worldly creatures that haunted the imaginations of the Israelites.

We learned in the last session that ancient temples often had carvings of large, animal-like statues symbolically guarding the entryway, in addition to actual soldiers. For example, the Sphinx in Egypt guarded the main road to the ancient pyramids, which were temple-tombs for kings who were considered gods. Ancient Babylonian temples were guarded by statues with eagles' wings and lions' bodies.

Well, the cherubim outside Eden were the real deal. This detail at the end of Genesis 3 is yet another indication that Eden was itself a temple, and that, by desecrating God's holy space, humans had been banished to a domain of their own.

Statues of cherubim appear later in God's temple in Jerusalem, where they were depicted as a combination of several animals, including lions, oxen, and eagles. This imagery suggests they were symbols of all creation. What made the cherubim statues in Jerusalem's temple distinct from their counterparts at other temples was their location. Instead of guarding the road or entrance to the temple, the cherubim were placed in the very center of the temple, their wings stretched over the ark of the covenant, which was considered the hot spot of God's presence.

Exodus 25:18–22 and 1 Kings 6:23–28 describe carvings of cherubim, and Ezekiel 1 and Isaiah 6 describe frightening encounters people had with them (in their dreams at least)!

Dig Deeper

Genesis 3 is the first time in the biblical narrative that God banished people—but it certainly wasn't the last. Let's examine a few Old Testament stories to see how banishment appears as a repeated theme throughout the biblical story.

1.

Read **Genesis 4:1–14**. Consider the significance of Cain's banishment occurring just one generation after Adam and Eve's banishment. Pay special attention to the similarities between **Genesis 3:24 and 4:14**.

2.

Read Moses' final words to the Israelites before they entered the Promised Land in **Deuteronomy 30:11–20**. How does the opportunity before Israel in the Promised Land mirror the choice before Adam and Even in the Garden?

3.

Read **Joel 2:3, Isaiah 51:3,** and **Ezekiel 36:33–36**. These prophets are all describing the ruined state of Israel after being conquered by enemies. Write down all the allusions to the Garden of Eden. How does the arden imagery reverse Israel's current tragedy?

Discussion

Share about a time in your life when you decided to define good and evil for yourself.
Did that decision lead to flourishing? Explain.

Share about a time when you decided to let God define good and evil for you. What came of that decision?

Do you think God overreacted by banishing humans from access to the garden temple?

How have you seen the theme of God's banishment play out in your life or the world today?

Notes

Session 4 | God's Rescue Mission

The Lord had said to Abram, "Go from your country, your people and your father's household to the land I will show you."

"I will make you into a great nation,
and I will bless you;
I will make your name great,
and you will be a blessing.
I will bless those who bless you,
and whoever curses you I will curse;
and all peoples on earth
will be blessed through you."

Genesis 12:1–3 (NIV)

After this, the word of the Lord came to Abram in a vision:

"Do not be afraid, Abram.
I am your shield,
your very great reward."

But Abram said, "Sovereign Lord, what can you give me since I remain childless and the one who will inherit my estate is Eliezer of Damascus?" And Abram said, "You have given me no children; so a servant in my household will be my heir."

Then the word of the Lord came to him: "This man will not be your heir, but a son who is your own flesh and blood will be your heir." He took him outside and said, "Look up at the sky and count the stars—if indeed you can count them." Then he said to him, "So shall your offspring be."

Genesis 15:1–5 (NIV)

Zooming Through History

After the story of the great split between God's domain and our domain, Genesis flies through human history. By Genesis 11, the population in ancient Mesopotamia had swelled into a civilization. At this point in the narrative, humans had recently innovated the mass production of bricks, which means they could build cities faster, stronger and taller than ever before.

Between fertile fields and new technology, humans got used to abundance pretty quickly. This led to a culture marked by arrogance—the same arrogance that prompted Adam and Eve to declare independence from God in the Garden. In Genesis 11, we see the human desire to be divine rear its ugly head in a big way.

See Genesis 11:4 to read about the arrogance of these people.

In their arrogance, these people set out to build a city called "Babylon" and construct "a tower whose top is in the heavens." They thought the tower would empower them to "make a name for [them]selves." This, of course, was the tower of Babel.

The tower of Babel was a massive architectural structure called a *ziggurat*. Ziggurats were large pyramid-shaped temples with a staircase or ramp leading to a flat platform on top. In the flat deltas of eastern Mesopotamia, these high places were the closest people could get to the sky.

Notice the use of "the heavens" here. Remember, the Hebrew word literally means "the skies." They were building a tower so tall that the top was in the sky. But also recall that "the skies" was one of the most common ways ancient Israelites referred to the place where God lived and ruled. In the context of this story, the author is clear that the people weren't just building the tower for a good view; they were trying to reach the realm of the divine. If they couldn't experience the tree of life in the garden as a gift from God, perhaps, they thought, they could attain divinity on their own.

The Problem with the Tower

God was not happy about this building project. Not because humans might have actually succeeded in attaining divinity, but because, yet again, they were trying to be gods themselves.

So, he confused everyone's language, making it impossible for people to work together. They scattered into new groups, effectively banished from the city—just like Adam and Eve were banished for the same error earlier in the story. The author of Genesis even uses parallels in the language to ensure readers notice history repeating itself:

> *And the Lord said, "Look, they are one people, and they have all one language; and this is only the beginning of what they will do; nothing that they propose to do will now be impossible for them. Come, let us go down, and confuse their language there, so that they will not understand one another's speech." So the Lord scattered them abroad from there over the face of all the earth, and they left off building the city.*
>
> Genesis 11:6–8 (NRSV)

In Genesis 11, the word "Babel" is playfully related to the Hebrew word *balal* which means "confusion." We'll talk about this more in the Geek Out section.

> *Then the Lord God said, "Look, the man has become like one of us, knowing good and evil; and now, he might reach out his hand and take also from the tree of life, and eat, and live forever"— therefore the Lord God sent him forth from the garden of Eden, to till the ground from which he was taken.*
>
> Genesis 3:22–23 (NRSV)

The rebellion in Babylon replayed the rebellion in the garden, but on a much wider scale. Despite the abundance of their cities, humans were still not content to be images of God. They wanted to claim power and honor for themselves. And, once again, God banished them. But this, of course, was not even close to the end of the story. In his judgment, God planted a seed of redemption.

Introducing Abram

Immediately after the story about the tower, the author launches into a genealogy that tracks a family affected by the scattering—the family of a man named Abram.

The introduction of Abram in Genesis 12 represents a big shift in the biblical story. Up to this point, the lens has been zoomed out to include the entire human race. Now, it zooms in on one man and the family that will come after him.

The story and genealogy of Abram's family is located in Genesis 11:10–32.

Abram's story marks the beginning of God's long-term strategic response to human rebellion, and the author of Genesis uses a few key words here to help readers understand how this new character fits into the bigger narrative. In Genesis 12:2, God says he will make

Abram's name great, which connects to Genesis 11:4, in which the people of Babylon attempted to make a name for themselves by building a tower. In contrast to humanity grasping at divine power for their own honor, God will grant the honor of a great name to this no-name family of Abram. God also says he will bless Abram, and what follows is a replay of God's blessing on Adam and Eve: a multiplying family, a fruitful land, and abundance.

Compare God's blessing to Abram in Genesis 12:1–3 with his blessing on humanity in 1:26–28.

To Abram, this promise was downright outlandish. He and his wife had never been able to have children, and they were already in their 70s. It seemed like God was maybe a tad too late. To make matters worse, God requested that Abram and Sarai leave their land. You can imagine Abram making a list of the hurdles that blocked the way to becoming a great nation: "No children, no land. Are you sure, God?"

But we're told that Abram was a man of radical faith, and he left his land despite those hurdles, trusting God implicitly. When the family arrived in Canaan, God gave him a new name—in effect, a new identity that reflected the promise he bore. He became *Abraham*.

Read about God renaming Abram in Genesis 17:1–8.

A Promise That Is a Gift

What makes God's commitment to Abraham truly remarkable was that the blessing served a strategic purpose: God promised that the blessing and abundance given to Abraham's family would overflow to all the other families of the earth. At that moment, Abraham's family became the carrier of the original blessing and vocation given to humanity in the garden so that every nation on earth might one day be reconnected to God.

"Through you (Abram), all the families of the earth will find blessing." (Genesis 12:3)

Now, Abraham and his family were not chosen because they were particularly great people. Many stories that follow highlight Abraham's frailty and his family's dysfunction. This reality makes a profound statement. Whatever the reunion of heaven and earth is going to be like, it won't be something humans achieve by their own power or deserve because of their own goodness.

Humans can't go back to the garden to get eternal life. They can't build up to the sky to attain it. No. Eternal life has only ever been possible as a gift. And that's precisely what God wants to give humanity. God wants his domain and our domain to completely overlap once more. To make this happen, he graciously calls an unlikely candidate to spearhead the project. God's plan through Abraham's family is to restore blessings to every nation on earth.

Geek Out

Babel = Babylon, Confusing!

Our English Bibles translate the name of the city and tower in Genesis 11 as "Babel." This is the Hebrew word babel that occurs 262 times in the Old Testament, and every other time it's translated "Babylon."

So why do all modern English translations render this word as "Babel" in Genesis 11? It's because of a clever Hebrew wordplay that's hard to reproduce in English.

We know that when the Babylonians got too cocky, God chose to confuse their language. The Hebrew word for "confuse" is *balal*, which sounds like "Babel." Here's the key line with its Hebrew transliteration to get the point across: "Therefore the city's name was called *babel* because there the Lord *balal* the language of the land." (Genesis 11:9)

Our English versions translate *babel* as "Babel" to honor the wordplay, but in so doing they obscure an even more important connection: This story is about the genesis of Babylon, the most infamous "bad guy" in the Old Testament.

Check out Isaiah's critique of the arrogant pride of the Babylonian rulers in Isaiah 14:5–17 and 47:5–15, and Jeremiah's description of Babylon as a super-human terror in Jeremiah 25 and 50–51.

After Babylon grew into an empire, it came to represent the worst of humanity's pride and rebellion. The Israelite prophets railed against the kings of Babylon, accusing them of having delusions of grandeur. The empire is later responsible for the Israelites' exile and was described as a larger-than-life enemy. The legacy of Babylon even lived on after the empire collapsed in 539 B.C. Much later, in the New Testament, Peter called Rome "Babylon" in a letter to churches experiencing persecution from the Romans. And in the final book of the Bible, the Revelation, all the nations unified against God are called "Babylon."

You can also see Peter and John's references in 1 Peter 5:13 and Revelation 17–18.

The story in Genesis 11 shows how pride was at the center of Babylon's roots.

Geek Out

Abraham's Name

When we first meet Abram in Genesis 11:26, his name means "exalted father." In Hebrew, his name consisted of two parts:

ab = father, *ram* = exalted

But then Abram got a new name, and the selection is surprisingly playful.

In Genesis 17:5 (NRSV), God said, "your name shall be Abraham; for I have made you the ancestor of a multitude of nations."

There are two things happening here, and the first is so simple we tend to overlook it completely. As a sign of his promise to "increase your numbers," God increases the syllables in Abram's name.

The second part of the wordplay isn't apparent in English. The Hebrew word for "multitude" is *hamon*. God takes the first letter of the word for "multitude" and sticks it into Abram's name, like this:

*ab-ram —> ab-ra**h**am*

So, Abraham's new name is actually the result of a Hebrew wordplay: God increases the length of his name by adding the first letter of the word for "multitude."

Dig Deeper

God's promise to Abraham is not just a promise to one man and his family. It's a promise to humanity that God is on a rescue mission. Let's take a look at how this promise reappears throughout Scripture.

1.

Read the following Scriptures, in which God promises to bless Abraham. Write down the exact promises God makes.

a. **Genesis 12:2**
b. **Genesis 17:5–8**
c. **Genesis 18:18–19**
d. **Genesis 22:15–18**

2.

Israel's prophets promised a day when people from all nations would become part of God's covenant people. Read the following passages and note how the prophets describe this promised day.

a. **Isaiah 2:1–6** and **56:3–8**
b. **Zechariah 8:20–23**
c. **Micah 4:1–3**

3.

Read **Jeremiah 31:31–34** and **Ezekiel 36:23–32**, where the prophets foretell that God would create a new covenant people. Then, read **Luke 22:14–23**, where Jesus claims to fulfill this prophecy. What similarities do you see?

4.

Read **Galatians 3** and **Romans 4**. Notice that the Apostle Paul firmly believed God's new family was not defined by ethnic lineage from Abraham anymore. Rather, God's people were identified as those who share Abraham's faith.

Discussion

In what ways do humans today use technology as a means to make ourselves like God?

Has God ever disrupted a project of yours in order to protect you from yourself?

As followers of Jesus, Paul would define us as spiritual children of Abraham. If God's plan is to reunite heaven and earth through Abraham's family, then what does that mean for you?

Notes

Session 5 | An Unexpected Encounter

Jacob left Beer-sheba and went toward Haran. He came to a certain place and stayed there for the night, because the sun had set. Taking one of the stones of the place, he put it under his head and lay down in that place. And he dreamed that there was a ladder set up on the earth, the top of it reaching to heaven; and the angels of God were ascending and descending on it. And the Lord stood beside him and said,

> *"I am the Lord, the God of Abraham your father and the God of Isaac; the land on which you lie I will give to you and to your offspring; and your offspring shall be like the dust of the earth, and you shall spread abroad to the west and to the east and to the north and to the south; and all the families of the earth shall be blessed in you and in your offspring. Know that I am with you and will keep you wherever you go, and will bring you back to this land; for I will not leave you until I have done what I have promised you."*

Then Jacob woke from his sleep and said, "Surely the Lord is in this place—and I did not know it!" And he was afraid, and said, "How awesome is this place! This is none other than the house of God, and this is the gate of heaven."

So Jacob rose early in the morning, and he took the stone that he had put under his head and set it up for a pillar and poured oil on the top of it. He called that place Bethel; but the name of the city was Luz at the first. Then Jacob made a vow, saying, "If God will be with me, and will keep me in this way that I go, and will give me bread to eat and clothing to wear, so that I come again to my father's house in peace, then the Lord shall be my God, and this stone, which I have set up for a pillar, shall be God's house; and of all that you give me I will surely give one-tenth to you."

Genesis 28:10–22 (NRSV)

God's Domain Is Chasing Us

The story known as "Jacob's ladder" is among the most popular Old Testament narratives—right up there with the parting of the Red Sea and Daniel's survival in the lions' den. And, like many other popular stories, its richness often gets lost as it's boiled down, over and over, into a children's story.

If you grew up in the church, your memory of this story might go something like this: Jacob, who once conned his brother out of the first-born inheritance, goes on a trip and apparently does not pack anything that will work as a pillow. He manages to fall asleep with his head on a rock, and has a wild dream about angels going up and down a flight of stairs between earth and heaven. Then he wakes up and pours some oil on the rock and gives it a name.

What in the world?

First things first, we know from the Hebrew words used in the text that what Jacob saw was a large stone staircase, not a ladder with rungs. In fact, what he saw was likely very similar to the massive stairways found on ancient temples that led up to the platforms where worshippers sought connection with their god.

But in Jacob's dream, the staircase was not attached to a temple—at least, not to a building. It was just stairs resting on earth, extending up to the skies. The meaning of this was clear to Jacob: This thing was a bridge, so to speak, between God's domain and humanity's domain. It was a pathway into God's heavenly throne room. "This is the gate of heaven," Jacob said. The angels, who were God's messengers, were going up and down the stairway, showing that this place was a kind of portal between heaven and earth.

Check this out in Genesis 28:17.

The God of his grandfather, Abraham, was following Jacob around and had revealed his divine presence out in the middle of nowhere. This was a God who chases people around.

Jacob's Role in the Story of Two Domains

It's a good thing God was committed to pursuing Jacob, because Jacob hadn't exactly led a life of devotion to his Creator. He was known as a deceiver, and earlier in life had tricked his blind father into giving him the family inheritance that should have been for his older brother.

Fortunately, the role of Abraham's family was not to be a model of upright behavior, but to carry divine blessings to the rest of the world. Apparently, God likes using insufficient people to do his work. It's a reminder that God does not need us to succeed, but rather that he succeeds despite us.

The key takeaway from Jacob's dream is that, somehow, God's domain and the human domain still overlap, that heaven chases people and touches down in the most unlikely of places. Jacob thought the spot where he was sleeping was a mundane space, but his vision helped him see that there was much more going on. This story is about how the presence of God, which we thought was left behind in the garden, comes bursting into the wilderness. There had been a rift between heaven and earth, and we no longer had access to God's presence, yet there it was.

Jacob's encounter shows that God was on a mission to reunite heaven and earth, that God was still among humans if they had eyes to see it—which is still true today. The story teaches us that God's character and his movement in our lives are often surprising. Heaven is at work much more than we probably realize. This is a gift, if we have eyes to see it.

Geek Out

Bethel

Jacob had this incredible encounter with God, and, in response, he did something that strikes modern readers as really odd: He took the stone he'd used as a pillow, propped it up, poured oil on it, and named the place Bethel.

Other Israelite memorial markers include Rachel's tomb (see Genesis 35:20), and Joshua's renewal of the covenant with Israel. (see Joshua 24:25- 27)

Setting up a stone pillar as a memorial marker was common cultural practice in the ancient world. And, actually, it still is today, though our modern memorials are polished and professionally engraved with explanations.

Read about the origins of Israel's sacred anointing oil in Exodus 30:22–29.

Pouring oil on something or someone was also common. It was a way to consecrate or set something aside for service in Israel's temple. This ritual could set apart people or items, like a memorial stone.

While the story in Genesis 28 doesn't give any details about Jacob's intent, his actions seem to fit those patterns of commemoration and sacred dedication.

Read about the temple of Bethel in 1 Kings 12:29–33.

What the text does highlight is that Jacob named the location "Bethel," which means "house of God" in Hebrew. This story connects with an important moment later in Israel's history when an Israelite temple was built in this same spot. The author of Genesis is telling an origin story for the temple of Bethel.

Angels

A key part of Jacob's dream about the stairs uniting heaven and earth are the figures going up and down it. They're called "angels," or in Hebrew, *mal'akim*, which simply means "messenger." The word can refer to any kind of messenger, human or divine, which opens up a fascinating can of worms.

The word "angel" is actually the Greek word (*angelos*) spelled with English letters. It means "messenger," and the first Jewish scholars who translated the Hebrew Bible into Greek used the Greek *angelos* to translate *mal'akim*.

At this point in the story of two domains, humans didn't have the option to enter God's personal presence. They could pray. They could see visions of God and hear from him, but they couldn't experience his presence as it was in the garden. In the next session, we'll see God remedy this situation by establishing a mobile tent-temple where humans can enter his presence, at least on a limited basis.

Read about the origins of Israel's sacred anointing oil in Exodus 30:22–29.

Geek Out

Angels (cont.)

But what if God wanted to reach out to someone who wasn't looking for him? On a handful of occasions in the Bible, God appears as a human who walks and talks with people, as in the story of God having a meal with Abraham. Sometimes, God sends a human messenger to carry a divine announcement on his behalf. In Israel, these figures were called prophets, and they acted as God's spokespeople. And even though it's strange to our ears, the prophets were often called God's angels, that is, his *mal'akim*. One of them was even called "my messenger," or in Hebrew, *mal'aki* (we know him as "Malachi").

But there's a third way that God could reach out to people. It's one step removed from a personal appearance, but it's more direct than sending a prophet. This is our traditional concept of angels, God's heavenly messengers. They're not human, but they're not God either. They share characteristics of both. They are creatures who inhabit God's domain, and essentially they serve as his executive staff team. Sometimes, they simply carried messages; other times, they performed miracles

If temples were inanimate, symbolic spaces that bridged heaven and earth, then angels were their animate counterparts. Sometimes in the Bible, these figures are simply called "a man." Other times, they are called "an angel" or "a messenger," and occasionally, they are called "sons of God," or even "gods."

The existence of these creatures that live in God's domain raises many questions that the biblical authors never address. How many are there? When were they created? How exactly do they bridge heaven and earth? Do they relate to our space-time dimensions the same way we do? The Bible offers no answers, mainly because it is focused on the function of angels instead of their nature or origins. What mattered to the author of the story about Jacob's "stairway" in Genesis was that the angels showed heaven and earth were interconnected.

Dig Deeper

Jacob wasn't the only biblical character to get an unexpected visit from God. Let's look at three other surprise encounters that demonstrate God's habit of showing up at unlikely times and places.

1.

Read Moses' encounter with God at the burning bush in **Exodus 3**. Observe similarities between this story and Jacob's dream. Notice in **verse 5** how the space around the bush is called "holy ground," as in physical space that is marked by God's presence.

2.

Read the story about Joshua near Jericho in **Joshua 5:13–15**.

3.

Check out the encounter Moses and the elders of Israel have with God's presence on Mt. Sinai in **Exodus 24:1–18**. Notice the similar language and imagery that appear in all these stories, and pay attention to what's different. Clouds, smoke, fire, and light are all featured in these moments where heaven and earth meet. What is the significance of this common imagery?

Discussion

Share a moment, however ordinary, in your story where you unexpectedly encountered God.

How has the God of Abraham pursued you in your life?

In what ways have you seen God use unlikely circumstances in your life to reveal himself?

| Notes

Session 6 | The Tabernacle

For generations to come this burnt offering is to be made regularly at the entrance to the tent of meeting, before the Lord. There I will meet you and speak to you; there also I will meet with the Israelites, and the place will be set apart as holy by my glory. I will set apart as holy the tent of meeting and the altar and I will set apart Aaron and his sons to serve me as priests. Then I will dwell among the Israelites and be their God. They will know that I am the Lord their God, who brought them out of Egypt so that I might dwell among them. I am the Lord their God.

Exodus 29:42–46

There, above the cover between the two cherubim that are over the ark of the covenant law, I will meet with you and give you all my commands for the Israelites.

Exodus 25:22 (NIV)

God Rescues Abraham's Family

For the purposes of this study, we're going to breeze past the Israelites' famous exodus from Egypt and spend time, instead, with the Israelites in the wilderness as they experienced God's presence in a new way.

For context, though, here's what you need to know: Jacob had a lot of children, and those children had a lot of children. Within just a few generations, Abraham's descendants grew into a small nation. After they had lived in Egypt for some time, Pharaoh decided to make them all slaves to the native Egyptians. God appointed an ineloquent murderer named Moses to lead an extraction operation; then rained plagues on Egypt until Pharaoh agreed to let the Israelites go. When Pharaoh changed his mind and had his soldiers pursue the Israelites, God parted a sea for his people and drowned their captors.

See Exodus 1–14 for the full story.

After some time in the wilderness, God formalized his promise to the family of Abraham with an ancient kind of agreement called a covenant. God gave the Israelites rules to live by that touched their business practices, how they treated the land, what they ate and wore, and how they handled disputes. In return for their obedience, God reasserted his promise to make them a great, blessed nation.

God Formalizes His Promise and Presence

At this point in the story, God gives Israel the blueprints to build an elaborate tent, which would serve as a type of temple. This tent paved the way for the Israelites to experience God's presence in a radical way. It effectively created a consistent overlap between heaven and earth after humanity was banished from the garden.

Up to this point, Abraham's descendants hadn't had their own temple. They were very familiar with the holy sites—Egypt had impressive ones, after all—but no Israelite had been able to seek the divine presence the way their neighbors did.

That changed in the book of Exodus. God gave the Israelites a blueprint for a mobile temple called "the tent of meeting," or "tabernacle," which was to be the place where God's glory and personal presence took up residence in the middle of Israel. Instead of only encountering God's presence through experiences like Jacob's dream, the Israelites would have consistent access to God as they roamed in the wilderness.

The Hebrew word for "tabernacle" is *mishkan*. It's the noun form of the verb *shakan*, "to dwell or inhabit." From this word comes the noun *shekinah*, which refers to God's glorious presence that dwelled in the holy space.

The Tabernacle: A Mobile Garden

Exodus includes detailed instructions as to how to build the tabernacle. These sections are really boring for most readers, but buried in the weeds of technicalities are some significant details.

First, the tabernacle was to be set up in the center of Israel's camp and built of the finest materials. The curtains were to be held up by golden posts, and the whole space was to be decorated with gold, silver, brass, animal skins, furs, and jewels. All of this fanciness symbolized something profound. Hosting the Creator God was one of the greatest privileges you could imagine, like hosting a king. The only materials fitting for such an honor are the ones listed in Exodus 25. This was to be a tent like no other.

Second, all the embroidery and metalwork in the tabernacle were to depict garden images. Entering the tabernacle was supposed to feel like entering a garden. The connection to the first and second chapters of Genesis couldn't be more clear. The tabernacle was a symbolic recreation of the garden temple in Eden, where God and humanity once dwelled together. Though God had banished humans from his presence in the garden temple, he used the tabernacle to station that same divine presence right in the middle of Abraham's family.

Read Exodus 25:31–40 and Exodus 28:31–35 for examples of the garden imagery found in the tabernacle.

The tabernacle was truly a gift. God's presence was not somewhere else, far away in the skies or in another land. No, now God would dwell among his people once more. They could build their lives around the rituals that connected them with their God. They could see it and smell it and think about it every day. God's presence filled the tabernacle, and fire and smoke hovered about the ark, guiding the Israelites through the wilderness.

The Problem With the Tabernacle

The tabernacle brought God's presence to the Israelites, but it also generated some tension. Remember, the reason for the rift between heaven and earth was humanity's rebellion in the Garden and in Babylon. As a result, God's plan to come and live among the Israelites, as he had in the garden, had to address that problem. God's presence may be accessible now, but that access was limited and dangerous.

Average Israelites could visit the outer court of the tabernacle, but first they had to sacrifice vital possessions, such as grain, wine, or livestock. They also had to undergo certain purity rituals, such as bathing and abstaining from touching things associated with death.

At the heart of these rituals was understanding the rift between God's domain and our domain. God's space was divine, pure, holy, and the source of all life. But human space was not. It was often the total opposite of all those things. If Israelites wanted to come close to the divine presence, they had to mark themselves as holy through the purification process.

Repeating a word, as in "Holy of Holies," is a Hebrew way of adding emphasis (think of "King of Kings" or "Song of Songs"). To call a place the "Holy of Holies" indicated it was the holiest place imaginable.

Even then, average Israelites did not have access to the hot spot of God's presence, which was a room at the center of the tabernacle called "the Holy of Holies." Only priests were allowed to enter this room, and only once a year. Priests were a special group of people whose role was to represent the entire Israelite community before God. This important job required attention to ritual details and a lifestyle of complete holiness. And the stakes were high. Being in proximity to God's holiness was like being close to the sun. If you don't follow procedure, you're going to get hurt. And a handful of priests who didn't follow protocol paid the price with their lives.

See Leviticus 10.

The Tabernacle as a Sign of New Creation

See Exodus 19:6.

This new access to God—however limited—was really good news to the Israelites. But remember, this story isn't just about them. God's plan was to bless all the nations and reunite all of heaven and earth through this family of Abraham.

The tabernacle was just the beginning of God's invasion of human space. It was a small, limited pocket of heaven on earth that symbolized God's intention to fill the whole earth with his unlimited presence and glory.

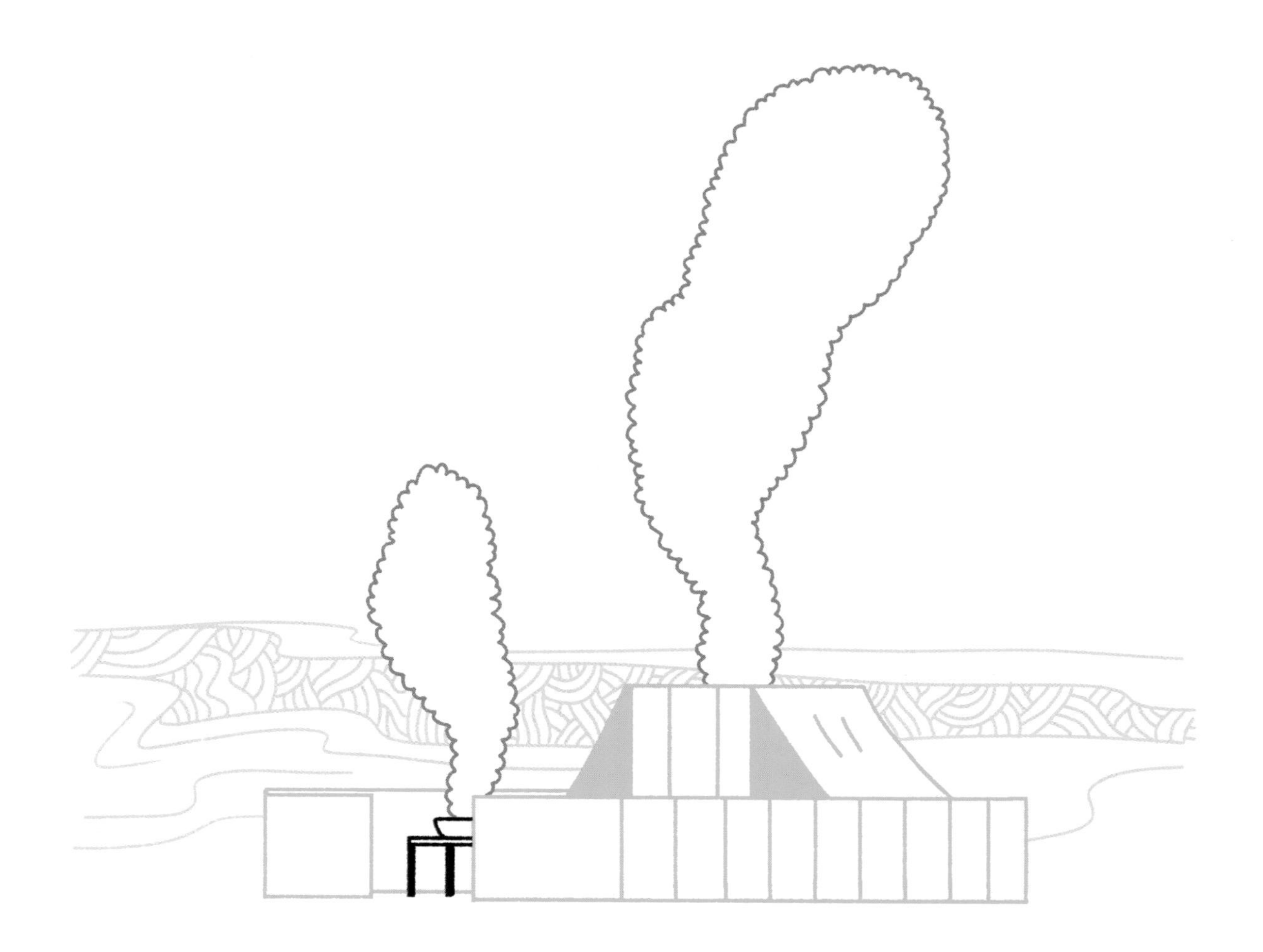

Geek Out

Israel's Priests

Read about the priestly family and the requirements they had to meet in Leviticus 8–10 and 21–22.

Another important aspect of the tabernacle was the personnel team that performed all the important rituals. We call them "priests." In Hebrew, they were called *kohanim*. They were real people—Aaron and his descendants—but their role was much larger than their individual identities.

This small team represented all of Israel before God, and their role required a unique way of life that set them apart to work in God's holy presence. Israel's priests were required to live by extremely high standards of ritual purity. They were to avoid contact with anything associated with death or decay, such as mold or dead bodies. They had to maintain a perpetual state of holiness.

"Say to Aaron: 'For the generations to come none of your descendants who has a defect may come near to offer the food of his God.'" (Leviticus 21:16)

Their actual bodies were symbols, too. To qualify as a priest, you had to be a descendant of Aaron and could not have any physical disabilities or misshapen features.

This goes against the grain of the modern western view of the universe. Doesn't the image of God in every human make them of equal value before God? Yes, and amen! That is a deeply biblical idea found in the book of Genesis. However, to impose that concept upon the priesthood is to miss the cultural symbolism.

The role of the priests was to be representatives, and they were to be symbols or "ideal" humans. In their culture, that was embodied by a priest whose body was without deformity of any kind. Modern western cultures have a different definition of the ideal human—one that does not exclude a person with physical disabilities. But God revealed himself to them in the context of their culture, not ours. Just as Israelite temples were embedded in ancient eastern culture, so were their priests. God wasn't endorsing their culture as superior; rather, he was meeting Israel on their terms and revealing himself to them through cultural vehicles that made sense.

The role of Israel's priests also spoke to a bigger, deeper issue in the biblical story. If God's domain and humanity's domain were ever to be fully joined again, humans needed some kind of mediator, a go-between who could represent humanity in its most ideal state. We needed a human who fulfills God's calling and purpose for humanity, and who could represent God to us. This is precisely the way the earliest Christians thought about Jesus, as the ultimate priest and mediator. In Jesus, we see perfect humanity as well as perfect deity, combined in one wise and loving person.

The concept of Jesus as a high priest permeates the New Testament book of Hebrews, especially chapters 5–10.

The Literary Location of Leviticus

The construction of the tabernacle begins in Exodus 25 and extends all the way to the end of the book. The only story found in this sea of architectural blueprints is the sad story of Israel's idolatry in making and worshipping a golden calf idol. After that tragedy, we come to the construction of the tent, and you would think this should be awesome. And it is. It's the glorious moment when God comes to live among his people. But what happens? Moses, the main character and Israel's representative before God, cannot enter the space. How anticlimactic! Israel's sin in casting the golden calf created yet another rift between heaven and earth, and it got in Moses' way.

The story of the golden calf is found in Exodus 32–34.

For Moses' inability to enter the tabernacle, see Exodus 40:35–40.

The next book in the Bible is Leviticus, and we see that Moses is outside the tent in the first sentence. This is not surprising, given how Exodus concluded. But turn to the next book, Numbers, and you'll see Moses has been allowed inside the tabernacle. How did that happen?

"And the Lord called to Moses and spoke to him **from** the tent..." (Leviticus 1:1).

"And the Lord spoke to Moses in the wilderness of Sinai, **in** the tent..." (Numbers 1:1).

The book of Leviticus, my friends! It's a big, complex book that's full of rituals and laws that are utterly bizarre to modern readers. But pay attention to the fact that this intimidating book provided a remedy for Israel's sin. This is the book's main contribution to the larger biblical narrative. Those odd rituals are God's way of reminding Israel that he is committed to them and to forgiving their failures.

See our website for a video about Leviticus: www.jointhebibleproject.com

Dig Deeper

This story about the tabernacle is a major milestone in the larger narrative of two domains of heaven and earth. God formalizes his covenant with Abraham, takes up residence among the people of Israel for the first time, and establishes a host of laws and rituals that follow Israel for thousands of years. When Jesus appeared on the scene, he and his followers drew upon the images and ideas associated with the tabernacle to describe what he was all about. Understanding the covenant, the tabernacle, and the priesthood is crucial for seeing how the entire biblical story fits together.

1.

First, read **Exodus 19:1–6**. What does it mean for Israel to be a "kingdom of priests" or "priestly kingdom"? How do the laws spelled out in **Exodus 20–23** help in this calling? Then read **1 Peter 2:9–10** and notice how Peter quotes from **Exodus 19**. Who are the priests now, and what is the purpose of their calling?

2.

Read **Hebrews 9–10**. There's a lot of detail here, but write down all the details about the Israelite tabernacle that, parallel with what Jesus accomplished in his death and resurrection. How do the parallels help you understand why Jesus died?

3.

Read **Matthew 4:23–25** and **Matthew 5:13–16**. Jesus came announcing God's kingdom and called his followers to "good works" for others to see. How is this connected to God's covenant with Israel?

4.

Read **1 Peter 1:13–16 and 2:9–10**. Notice how Peter uses the language of the tabernacle and priesthood to describe this same vocation of Jesus' followers. Why is this significant?

| Discussion

What do you consider God's most meaningful promises to his people? What promises do you rest in?

In 1 Peter 2:9, the Apostle Peter tells Christians scattered all over the Greek world that, just like ancient Israel, they are a chosen people and a royal priesthood. How is this identity meaningful for you?

What rituals and traditions do you have that remind you of God's presence?

Notes

Session 7 | God's Confusing Presence

Look down from heaven, your holy dwelling place, and bless your people Israel…

Deuteronomy 26:15 (NIV)

Lord, our Lord, how majestic is your name in all the earth! You have set your glory in the heavens.

Psalm 8:1 (NIV)

But will God really dwell on earth? The heavens, even the highest heaven, cannot contain you. How much less this temple I have built!

1 Kings 8:27 (NIV)

Thus says the Lord:
Heaven is my throne
and the earth is my footstool;
what is the house that you would build for me,
and what is my resting place?

Isaiah 66:1 (NRSV)

Where Does God Live?

The tabernacle was a major turning point in the story of God's mission to reunite his domain and our domain. It was the first time since the garden that God's presence was consistently accessible to his people, and, even though that access was extremely limited, this was an exciting and miraculous thing. God now lived among Israel in the tabernacle.

But remember the first session, where we looked at many biblical texts that associated God's presence with the sky. The idea of the sky, or the heavens, as God's domain is found from the beginning to the end of the Bible, alongside the idea that God's presence is in the tabernacle.

This creates some confusion. Did the Israelites believe God lived in the tabernacle or in the sky? Was God's presence in the tabernacle only symbolic, or was God's presence actually stronger in the tabernacle than it was anywhere else?

In this session, we're taking a break from the narrative about the reunion of heaven and earth to explore the fascinating question of where God lives.

What the Ancient Israelites Thought

We know ancient Israelites associated God's presence with the sky because of shared qualities, such as vastness, majesty, power, and mystery. But it's not so clear that they believed that's where their God actually lived. It's more likely that all of this "sky" imagery is a statement about God's status and authority rather than a claim about God's actual location.

What we know for sure is that the biblical authors didn't think God dwelled *only* in the sky. As we established in the previous session, they also believed God dwelled in the tabernacle. Israelites also knew God could appear on earth outside the tabernacle in surprising moments, such as when he spoke to Moses through a burning bush or visited Jacob in a dream.

Beyond using physical metaphors to reflect God's character, biblical authors rarely addressed God's location. However, a key passage in 1 Kings sheds light on how King Solomon conceived of God's presence.

Many years after the establishment of the tabernacle—after the Israelites made it to the Promised Land, and after David killed Goliath and became king—a king named Solomon oversaw the construction of a truly glorious temple. The temple was crafted from marble with gold and silver embellishments. It had bronze pillars and cedar paneling. It was Solomon's crowning achievement and a huge upgrade from the tabernacle, which the Israelites had used up to that point.

Solomon was David's son. Because David was responsible for so much bloodshed, God did not allow him to build a temple (see 1 Kings 5:3 and 1 Chronicles 22:8–10). Solomon, however, ruled in a time of peace, which allowed him to focus on this building project.

When the temple was complete, 1 Kings 8:10–11 tells us God's presence came in the form of a great cloud to take up residence there. Then, Solomon makes a surprising statement:

> *"But will God really dwell on earth? The heavens, even the highest heavens, cannot contain you. How much less this temple I have built!"*
>
> 1 Kings 8:27 (NIV)

Solomon believed the divine presence was too magnificent for his temple or even for the vast and majestic skies.

Solomon wasn't alone in this sentiment. In Isaiah 66, the prophet claimed no house could hold God because God had made all things. Psalm 139 includes one of the most beautiful expressions of this belief in the entire Bible:

> *Where can I go from your Spirit?*
> *Where can I flee from your presence?*
> *If I go up to the heavens, you are there;*
> *if I make my bed in the depths, you are there.*
>
> Psalm 139:7–8 (NIV)

So, while we don't know for sure what most ancient Israelites believed about the location of God's presence, we do know that a number of leaders clearly considered his glory too great to be limited to the sky or the tabernacle.

If God Is Everywhere, Why a Temple?

God's presence in all of creation doesn't cancel out the fact that God came to the tabernacle and, later, to the temple in Jerusalem in a unique way. The biblical authors don't ever explain how that works in detail; they just claim that this is the case. Of course, the Creator God is present in all of his creation, and of course the God of Israel lives among his people in a special way. And because the Creator *is* the God of Israel, these two claims about his presence sit alongside each other without much explanation.

Even if the Israelites couldn't explain exactly how God could be present everywhere and right there in the temple, the divine presence was a source of confidence and assurance for the Israelites—a reminder that he really was on their side. They could see the mysterious cloud hovering above it. They would even direct their prayers toward the temple, much as Muslims direct their prayers toward Mecca.

The people of Israel had a sacred habit of praying at fixed hours of the day, and the practice was to face the temple, no matter your location. Even Daniel, hundreds of miles away in Babylon, directed his prayers to the temple. (see Daniel 6:10)

But it was more than that. God's special presence in the tabernacle and the temple was a symbol of future hope—a promise that, one day, God's full and unlimited presence would fill all of creation. Though God was already everywhere, surely the Israelites sensed that his presence in creation wasn't what it could be, what it was meant to be. This special experience of the divine presence in the temple ought to be more accessible to more people than just those living in Jerusalem. The temple was a potent symbol of God's desire for heaven and earth to be reunited, and the Jerusalem temple was where it would start.

WHERE DOES GOD LIVE

- ☑ the skies
- ☑ on Earth
- ☑ the depths
- ☑ Solomon's temple
- ☑ above the skies
- ☑ anywhere possible I can go

So, let's tie all these ideas together. Did God live in the tabernacle and the temple? Yes, sort of. In the skies? Yes, sort of. Does he live everywhere? Yes, also, sort of. God is not contained or limited to any of those spaces, but each one conveys a specific meaning about his presence. The skies tell us God is King of all. His presence out in creation tells us God is Creator of all. And his presence in the temple tells us he stubbornly created and maintained an overlap between heaven and earth despite human rebellion. Together, these focal points of his presence foreshadow a day when a new king will reunite all of heaven and earth and flood all creation with God's glorious presence.

Geek Out

The Highest Heavens

Think back to the first session when we learned about the three-tiered view of the universe.

Here's a recap: Ancient people perceived the universe as broken into three distinct tiers. At the bottom was water—one giant, chaotic ocean. In the middle was land, which they imagined as a disc floating in the ocean. On top was the sky, which was encompassed by a dome in which the sun, moon, and stars were embedded. "Heavens" or "heavens above" referred to the space extending up to the dome.

With this in mind, let's look back at Solomon's prayer of dedication of the temple in Jerusalem: "But will God really dwell on earth? The heavens, even the highest heavens, cannot contain you. How much less this temple I have built!"

See 1 Kings 8:27 (NIV).

What does he mean by "the highest heavens"? In Hebrew, the phrase he uses is literally "the heavens of the heavens," or "the skies of the skies." In a three tiered universe, the highest place visible to humans was the dome itself. Solomon stretched that worldview, saying that God, as the exalted King, must be present in the abyss above and beyond the dome. And even this space, according to Solomon, is not grand enough or big enough to contain all of God's holiness and transcendence. He was pushing his concept of the universe to its limit.

See also Deuteronomy 10:14: "To the Lord belong the heavens, and the heavens of the heavens, the land and everything on it."

This concept of the heavens above the heavens shows up in the New Testament, too, in Paul's letter to the Corinthians. In 2 Corinthians 12, Paul describes incredible visions he saw about Jesus enthroned above all creation, visions that were remarkably similar to what John describes in Revelation. Paul's language for explaining what he saw is fascinating. He says this vision took him "up to the third heaven," which he later calls "paradise." If the furthest extent of Solomon's universe was the "heavens of the heavens," Paul goes one step further: the heavens of the heavens of the heavens!

"I know a man in Christ who…was caught up to the third heaven…was caught up to paradise and heard inexpressible things." (2 Corinthians 12:2–4)

The Greek word *paradeiso* is the standard term to refer to the garden of Eden in the ancient Greek translation of the Old Testament, and in Jesus' words to the thief on the cross. (see Luke 23:43)

And what word does Paul use to describe this marvelous throne room in the heavens above the heavens above the heavens? In our English translations, we see "paradise." But in Greek? The word means "garden." The triple-heavens, the transcendent throne room of God and Jesus, is none other that the paradise Garden of Eden, where God and Humanity live together in perfect harmony.

Dig Deeper

Before we resume the story of two domains, let's explore a few places in the Bible where the authors grapple with the complexity of God's presence.

1.

Read **Isaiah 6,** in which the prophet has a vision of God in the temple. Notice Isaiah's descriptions of God's robe as filling the temple and heavenly creatures attending from above. Consider what this visual teaches about God's presence.

2.

Read **Psalm 72**, paying special attention to **verse 19**. How is this connected to God's mission to reunite heaven and earth? Who might the anticipated king be?

3.

Read **Habakkuk 2:14**. You might wonder, "Why does he say waters cover the sea? The waters are the sea!"
Reflect on this as a powerful metaphor of how God's presence will fully permeate creation someday.

| Discussion

How do you conceive of where God lives? Where does that idea come from?

Solomon believed there was no single place that could contain God. What does that conviction do to your perspective of the known universe?

Do you long for a time when God's presence will fill the whole earth? What do you imagine that will be like?

| Notes

Session 8 | The Prophetic Hope

"See, I will create
new heavens and a new earth.
The former things will not be remembered,
nor will they come to mind.
But be glad and rejoice forever
in what I will create,
for I will create Jerusalem to be a delight
and its people a joy.
I will rejoice over Jerusalem
and take delight in my people;
the sound of weeping and of crying
will be heard in it no more.
"Never again will there be in it
an infant who lives but a few
days, or an old man who does
not live out his years;
the one who dies at a hundred
will be thought a mere child;
the one who fails to reach a hundred
will be considered accursed.
They will build houses and dwell in them;
they will plant vineyards and eat their fruit.
No longer will they build houses and others live
in them,
or plant and others eat.
For as the days of a tree,
so will be the days of my people;
my chosen ones will long enjoy
the work of their hands.
They will not labor in vain,
nor will they bear children doomed
to misfortune;
for they will be a people blessed by the Lord,
they and their descendants with them.
Before they call I will answer;
while they are still speaking I will hear.
The wolf and the lamb will feed together,
and the lion will eat straw like the ox,
and dust will be the serpent's food.
They will neither harm nor destroy
on all my holy mountain,"
says the Lord.

Isaiah 65:17-25 (NIV)

Then you will know that I, the Lord your God,
dwell in Zion, my holy hill.
Jerusalem will be holy;
never again will foreigners invade her.

"In that day the mountains will drip new wine,
and the hills will flow with milk;
all the ravines of Judah will run with water.
A fountain will flow out of the Lord's house
and will water the valley of acacias.

Joel 3:17–18 (NIV)

In the last days
the mountain of the Lord's temple will be established
as the highest of the mountains;
it will be exalted above the hills,
and peoples will stream to it.
Many nations will come and say,
"Come, let us go up to the mountain of the Lord,
to the temple of the God of Jacob.
He will teach us his ways,
so that we may walk in his paths."
The law will go out from Zion,
the word of the Lord from Jerusalem.
He will judge between many peoples
and will settle disputes for strong nations far and wide.
They will beat their swords into plowshares
and their spears into pruning hooks.
Nation will not take up sword against nation,
nor will they train for war anymore.
Everyone will sit under their own vine
and under their own fig tree,
and no one will make them afraid,
for the Lord Almighty has spoken.

Micah 4:1–4 (NIV)

Review

Now that we've cleared up some confusion around God's whereabouts, we're going to dive back into the story of two domains. But first, let's review what happened before we took a break:

THE HEAVENS AS THE SKIES
God created the heavens and the earth, which is to say he created the skies and the land. We learned that biblical authors use "skies" and "clouds" to talk about God's domain or dwelling place.

THE GARDEN TEMPLE
God's divine presence dwelled fully with humanity in the garden temple of Eden. His domain and our domain were one.

THE GREAT SPLIT
Humans prioritized their own knowledge and power over God, choosing to define good and evil for themselves. God banished them from his garden temple, creating two separate and incompatible domains.

GOD'S RESCUE MISSION
God chose the family of Abraham to be carriers of the blessing he originally gave humans in the garden, promising to reunite heaven and earth through Abraham's descendants.

AN UNEXPECTED ENCOUNTER
Abraham's grandson, Jacob, learns through a wild dream that heaven can invade earth. We learned that God's space isn't entirely separated from our space, and that God pursues people he's committed to.

THE TABERNACLE
God formalized his promise to Abraham's family and came to dwell among them in a mobile temple called a tabernacle. This was the first long-term overlap between heaven and earth since Eden.

Israel Falls Apart

After the construction of the tabernacle, the Israelites continued to wander in the wilderness for decades. When they finally made it to the Promised Land, they victoriously fended off enemies and saw the reign of the famous Israelite kings, David and Solomon, who oversaw the construction of the temple in Israel.

Read about the split of the Israelite kingdoms in 1 Kings 11–12. For the destruction and exile of Israel, check out 2 Kings 24–25.

But after Solomon's death, conflict split the nation in two—Israel in the north, Judah in the south—and both kingdoms spiraled into internal meltdown. They utterly failed to keep the terms of the covenant, so God allowed foreign empires to conquer their land, destroy the temple, and take the Israelites into exile.

What? I thought this nation was going to play a role in the reunion of heaven and earth. But, instead, they no longer have their own land to call home, and the temple is destroyed. Did God give up on them? This is the question the Israelite prophets were intensely interested in.

The Prophetic Hope of New Creation

The books of the prophets make up nearly 25 percent of the entire Bible and nearly one third of the Old Testament.

The next stop in our quest to see Scripture through the lens of heaven and earth is the dense Hebrew poetry of the prophets. These books were written leading up to, during, and after the Israelites' exile from their land. These books are challenging to read, but crucial for understanding the biblical story and Jesus' role within it.

Prophets were people who had experienced God's presence in a unique way, like Jacob did through his dream at Bethel. And these unique moments marked the prophets and changed their lives forever. It resulted in a heightened awareness of God's presence and purpose. The prophets saw connections that other people didn't see, and they looked at Israel's history in a different way. They saw God's hand at work in the tragedy of Israel's exile, viewing defeat as God's way of punishing Israel for centuries of injustice and covenant rebellion.

The prophets didn't only speak of judgment and doom. They deeply believed that God was still going to fulfill his ancient promises to Abraham, despite Israel's failure. They preached a message of hope, that somehow God would still use Israel to bring his blessing to the world. They foresaw that God would fulfill the promise through a future king, the Messiah, who would lead the people back to God. The prophets promised that Israel would one day return to their ancestral land and rebuild the temple, so God could dwell among them once again.

They imagined this future time as an age of world peace and harmony, when all the nations would rally around Jerusalem, and they described God's presence as filling the earth in a special way. In short, they envisioned God's domain rejoining with our domain in a new creation—or, as Isaiah said, "new heavens and a new earth." (Isaiah 65:17)

Wading Through the Language

The language of the prophets is poetic, imaginative, and, frankly, really challenging for some modern readers. Wine dripping from mountains? Ferocious animals playing with babies? Weapons melted into farm equipment? Well, that last one is pretty cool.

The prophets were trying to describe the indescribable—a change in the nature of creation itself. The images are supposed to boggle your mind and break your categories. Poetry is the only kind of language appropriate to the strangeness and wonder of this renewed world.

Yet alongside fantastical images of milk streaming down hills, we also find scenes familiar to our own experience of this world, such as this one from Isaiah 65:21: "They will build houses and dwell in them; they will plant vineyards and eat their fruit."

That sounds normal, right? The prophets imagined a world that is like ours, but with all the good things preserved and the broken things renewed.

It's essential that we don't make this poetry do more than it's meant to. For instance, it's tempting to analyze whether Isaiah 65:20 ("The one who dies at a hundred will be thought a mere child; the one who fails to reach a hundred will be considered accursed") and ask why the prophet is talking about aging and death in the new creation. But that's the wrong question. The point is that life's limits as we experience them in our world will be broken through. New horizons will open up that were previously unimaginable. Turning 100 will be child's play. To make the passage say more that this, as if it's offering biological information, is to forget we're reading poetry.

Looking Ahead to Jesus

Understanding this prophetic hope of new creation is important because it's the same hope that Jesus and the apostles were raised with and embraced as their own.

Jesus' announcement that God's kingdom had arrived was based on this hope. When the apostles spread the word that Jesus had died and was raised from the dead, it was the fulfillment of this hope.

Jesus spoke of the "renewal of all things" in Matthew 19:28, and Peter announced that the "restoration of all things" would happen when Jesus returned (see Acts 3:19–21). In Romans 8:23, Paul's expressed hope is that "creation itself will be set free from its bondage to corruption."

In Jesus, God had finally acted again, moving the world one step closer to the new creation. It's a creation where heaven and earth come back together, a world that will be recognizable in some ways, and in others unimaginable.

Geek Out

Death: The Great Enemy

The tree of life in Genesis 2 represented proximity to God, the source and Creator of all life and beauty and joy. To be near him is to truly live, and so access to his presence is also access to eternal life.

In contrast, death (pronounced *mot* in Hebrew) is the ultimate tragedy and one of the sad realities of the split between God's domain and humans' domain. The whole point was for humans to receive the gift of life, but their rebellion was a sad forfeiture of God's generous offer.

This sense of tragedy is why the Old Testament offers such a rich and poetic portrayal of the grave. It's the anti-Eden, the opposite of God's desire for humanity.

The Hebrew word for "grave" is *she'ol*, the place to which humans descend upon death. But only rarely does it simply refer to dirt. More often, *she'ol* is described with poetic imagery that explores the meaning of death within the biblical story and within the three-tiered universe envisioned by the biblical authors.

There's an old debate about the original meaning of the Hebrew word *she'ol*. A common suggestion connects it to a similar Hebrew word *sha'al*, which means "ask" or "inquire." This word sometimes describes the ancient practice of necromancy, or asking the dead to predict the future, and so some scholars think *she'ol* means "the place for inquiring the dead."

Since death is the very opposite of God's desire to create life, the spatial location of the grave under the ground is often emphasized as a contrast to the heavens in the sky. If the heavens are God's space and if God is the source of life, then the grave must be the farthest place from the heavens. This is why the biblical poets sometimes talk about "the depths of the earth" as the realm of the dead.

Not only is the grave at the opposite end of the cosmos in relation to God's domain in the heavens, but it also stands for the opposite of the delights and joys that come with God's presence. *She'ol* is the ultimate pointless, painful conference that never ends. The biblical authors describe *she'ol* as a place where people can't praise God or even speak at all. In *she'ol*, everyone sleeps in regret and agitation.

For more on these details about *she'ol*, read Psalm 6:5, Psalm 31:17, Psalm 116:3, Ecclesiastes 9:10, and Isaiah 14:9-11.

Geek Out

For descriptions of the irreversible nature of the grave, see Psalms 49:7–9 and 89:47–48.

The most disturbing thing about death for the biblical poets was its inevitability and irreversible nature. In the view of the biblical authors, humanity was on a one-way path toward death unless God intervened. They knew that if humans were ever to recover the divine gift of immortality, it wouldn't be because humans fixed the problem. It would have to be a gift from heaven, which is exactly what's described in the book of Isaiah. Watch how God reverses the despair of the grave:

On this mountain the Lord Almighty
will prepare a feast of rich food for all peoples,
a banquet of aged wine—
the best of meats and the finest of wines.
On this mountain he will swallow up
the shroud that enfolds all peoples,
the sheet that covers all nations;
he will swallow up death forever.
The Sovereign Lord will wipe away the tears from all faces.

Isaiah 25:6–8 (NIV)

In contrast to the depths of *she'ol*, this scene is placed on a high mountain, as close to the heavens as humans could get. Notice that it's a great party, with loads of fine meats and wines. In contrast to *she'ol*, a place of quiet and sad deprivation, the new creation is permeated with abundance, joy, and celebration.

See Psalms 49:15 and 73:23–26.

You can find this same kind of hope expressed by the Israelite poets in the Psalms, in which the authors balanced their fear of death or suffering with their conviction that God is the good Creator. This results in powerful statements about God "redeeming" people from the grave.

See Daniel 12:1–4.

The book of Daniel also contains this hope. It was written during a dark time, when Israel was oppressed by foreign rulers, and many people were killed. The book concludes by offering hope for the faithful who have died, saying that one day they will wake up from the grave and find themselves alive in God's presence.

The point of all these poetic descriptions is not to speculate about the fate or experience of the dead. Rather, the writers were painting a vivid contrast: Death is the opposite of what God wants for humans. And they believed that someday God would do something about that. He would bring about the *death* of death.

Dig Deeper

The prophet Ezekiel seems to have been fascinated with the Garden of Eden. He mentions Eden repeatedly in his poetry, and much of his hope for renewed creation was inspired by the garden temple. Let's explore the garden imagery in his writings.

1.

Read **Ezekiel 28:13, 31:9,** and **36:35**. Note each time the prophet references the garden.

2.

In **Ezekiel 47,** the prophet has a vision of Jerusalem and the new temple restored after their destruction. Read this fantastic vision and then turn to **Genesis 2** and reread the description about the garden of Eden. What is similar in these passages? What is different? What's the significance of the distinctions?

3.

Read **John 4:1–14**. Note how Jesus turns this conversation about water into a conversation about himself as the source of eternal life. How do his metaphors draw upon the stories of sacred rivers in **Genesis 2** and **Ezekiel 47**?

| Discussion

What lines of poetry from this session were the most mind-boggling to you? What do you imagine the author was trying to convey?

What lines of poetry from this session resonated with you the most? Why?

What would be different about your life if, like the prophets, your hope was in the new creation?

Notes

Session 9 | Heaven Invading Earth

"The time has come," he said. "The kingdom of God has come near. Repent and believe the good news!"

Mark 1:15 (NIV)

This, then, is how you should pray:
"'Our Father in heaven,
hallowed be your name,
your kingdom come,
your will be done,
on earth as it is in heaven.
Give us today our daily bread.
And forgive us our debts,
as we also have forgiven our debtors.
And lead us not into temptation,
but deliver us from the evil one."

Matthew 6:9–13 (NIV)

Then Jesus asked, "What is the kingdom of God like? What shall I compare it to? It is like a mustard seed, which a man took and planted in his garden. It grew and became a tree, and the birds perched in its branches."

Again he asked, "What shall I compare the kingdom of God to? It is like yeast that a woman took and mixed into about sixty pounds of flour until it worked all through the dough."

Luke 13:18–21 (NIV)

Once, on being asked by the Pharisees when the kingdom of God would come, Jesus replied, "The coming of the kingdom of God is not something that can be observed, nor will people say, 'Here it is,' or 'There it is,' because the kingdom of God is in your midst."

Luke 17:20–21 (NIV)

For God was pleased to have all his fullness dwell in him, and through him to reconcile to himself all things, whether things on earth or things in heaven, by making peace through his blood, shed on the cross.

Colossians 1:19–20 (NIV)

Jesus' Favorite Topic

Jesus was a prophet, and his favorite topic was heaven and earth uniting. He used the phrase "the kingdom of God" to refer to this reality.

Just imagine you lived in Jesus' time. Word has spread that he is passing through your village, so you rush into town with everyone else. This is your one chance to hear him speak—your whole community's one chance.

What does he say? Knowing he may not visit your town again, what's the one message he prioritizes above everything else?

"The kingdom of God has arrived."

Today, Jesus is most often associated with his moral teachings, such as his command to love others as you love yourself, but that reputation is not actually a reflection of the message he valued most. To his contemporaries, Jesus was not viewed primarily as a moral teacher, but as a new prophet announcing that the long dormant promises of prophets like Isaiah were finally coming to pass. Heaven was aggressively invading earth, just as the prophets predicted—and Jesus presented himself as the one making it happen.

Once your radar is alerted to Jesus' core concern for the arrival of God's kingdom, you can't un-see it. It's everywhere. For instance, consider the Lord's Prayer. Jesus teaches his disciples to ask God to bring his kingdom to earth before they ask for anything else. Heaven invading earth was Jesus' top priority, and he wanted it to be the disciples' too.

What did it mean that the kingdom of God had arrived? Clearly, God had not thoroughly renewed all of creation. Yet, somehow, Jesus signaled a new arrival of God's domain overcoming and settling into our domain.

In Jesus, God began a full-throttle invasion of our domain. No longer was God's domain limited to the inner sanctum of the temple or short, dream-like visits to key Israelites. The general was on-site, and he was recruiting an army. This army was going to break down the gates of *she'ol*. Victory was unavoidable. Heaven and earth were going to unite.

An Unlikely Kingdom

What is the kingdom of heaven like? This invading kingdom—also called "the kingdom of heaven"—was, and is, fundamentally different from human kingdoms. Jesus repeatedly pointed to the Old Testament, reminding his listeners that Israel was the most successful when they were most dependent on God and least dependent on their own military, wit, or resources. Think of God's work through Abraham, the wandering and long-childless patriarch; through Gideon, a cowardly, army-less warrior; and through David, a no-name shepherd boy.

Jesus presented himself as the king the prophets had hoped for—the king bringing divine rule to Israel. But he would not bring his rule through military might or coercive power. Rather, Jesus taught that the most powerful members of his kingdom were the slaves and the rejects. God's kingdom is a strange one, where all of our normal ways of living and thinking are turned upside-down—or right-side up.

Mark 10:43–45: "Whoever wants to become great among you must be your servant, and whoever wants to be first must be the slave of all, for the Son of Man didn't come to be served, but to be a servant and give his life as a ransom for many."

That right-side-up reign of God exists fully in God's domain, and with the arrival of Jesus, it began moving into ours. Jesus taught his followers to pray every day that God's kingdom would advance farther into earth, that God's domain would reclaim more and more of humanity's domain.

The Kingdom Through Parables

When Jesus talked about the kingdom of God, he often did so through parables. Parables are short, fictional tales that help people understand challenging revelations about this right-side-up kingdom.

For the parable of the mustard seed, see Mark 4:30–32.

One day, Jesus told a parable about how the kingdom of God was like a tiny mustard seed that grew into a huge tree and became a home for many birds. This visual would have been very familiar to his audience, which was mostly made up of subsistence farmers and day laborers. They understood that even the tiniest seed had immense potential. They knew a single seed could nourish one bird for a few hours or grow into a tree that sheltered and fed thousands of birds.

Skeptical leaders were alson in the audience that day, inspecting Jesus and his movement. They were unimpressed with him and his ragtag entourage. And whether or not the leaders understood his meaning, Jesus had a message for them in this parable: It might look like a tiny seed now, but just wait. The kingdom of God has been planted, and it will grow.

The Kingdom Is Talking

On another occasion, some religious leaders asked Jesus when he thought God's kingdom would come. In their mind, the coming kingdom involved a political revolution that would liberate Israel from Roman rule. They assumed the arrival of the kingdom would be an unmissable event.

For this story, see Luke 17:20–21.

But Jesus told them they wouldn't notice the coming of God's kingdom. It would be inconspicuous, hidden in plain sight. Only those with eyes to see it would know. In fact, he said, they'd already missed it. The kingdom of God was "in their midst." This was a not-so-subtle way of pointing to himself and saying, "The kingdom is talking to you now."

Jesus believed he was inaugurating God's heavenly kingdom here on earth. He was initiating the reunion of God's domain and humanity's domain. He was the tiny seed. And with his band of a few hundred followers, God's kingdom was taking root.

Geek Out

"Kingdom" by the Numbers

"Kingdom" is one of the most frequent words Jesus speaks in the Gospels. Taking note of the word count is a lesson in itself:

THE GOSPEL OF MARK
Jesus brings up the kingdom of God nearly 20 times in chapters 1–14. (That's 1.5 times per chapter.)

LUKE'S GOSPEL
Jesus mentions God's kingdom nearly 45 times in chapters 4–22. (That's 2.5 times per chapter.)

MATTHEW
It is even more frequent. Jesus mentions the kingdom over 50 times in chapters 3–24. (That's 2.6 times per chapter.)

Of Heaven

In Matthew, Jesus not only talks about the kingdom more than in the other Gospels, but he also talks about it differently. Most often we find the phrase, "kingdom of heaven," instead of the more common phrase in Mark and Luke, "the kingdom of God."

It's no surprise to you at this point that "heaven" or "heavens" was a traditional way to talk about God's dwelling place or domain. But Matthew's choice of "kingdom of heaven" isn't just a linguistic preference. It's a subtle clarification.

According to Matthew, God wasn't simply establishing a brand-new rule on earth. He was bringing his existing rule in heaven (his domain) to earth (our domain).

You can see Matthew's point most clearly when you compare Jesus' first public words in Matthew 4:17, "the kingdom of heaven has come near," with his final words to the disciples in 28:18: "all authority in heaven and on earth has been given to me." From first to last, Matthew portrays Jesus as the one who brings God's heavenly kingdom here to earth.

Geek Out

The Present-Future Kingdom of God

An interesting puzzle that has exercised the imaginations of Bible readers for a long time is the diversity of the language Jesus used to talk about the kingdom of God.

In many of his teachings, it's clear that Jesus believed God's heavenly reign was a clear and present reality. He said it had "arrived" in himself, and that by following him and living by his teachings a person could "enter" or "see" or "seek" or even "receive" God's kingdom. These phrases indicate that God's heavenly reign is an earthly reality that can be experienced here and now.

See "enter" in Matthew 5:20, "seek" in Matthew 6:33, "see" in Mark 9:1, and "receive" in Mark 10:15.

But Jesus also talks about the kingdom as it if hasn't arrived yet—at least not completely. When he taught his disciples to pray, he said, "May your kingdom come," implying that it was not present, but future. He talked about his future return after the resurrection as "the Son of Man coming in his kingdom."

See Matthew 6:10 and 16:28.

So, which is it? Is the kingdom a present reality or a future hope? Is God's heavenly rule something that has invaded earth, or is it an impending promise?

It seems that Jesus' answer was "yes and yes." One minute Jesus portrays the kingdom as something you pray will come; then a few moments later he talks about the kingdom as something you can "seek" and "enter" in this moment by following him. Our stark either/or categories simply won't help us in explaining Jesus' vision of the heavenly kingdom.

New Testament scholars use the word "inauguration" as a metaphor to help us understand what's going on. In the ancient world, before telecommunications and Twitter, it took time for an entire empire to be notified that a new king was on the throne—and even longer for that king to personally visit each district. So, though a new king was technically an inaugurated ruler, it took a while for the kingdom to fully experience his rule in person. A theologian named George Eldon Ladd used the handy phrase "already and not yet" to capture the kingdom's dual present and future reality.[2]

George Ladd's important book on the presence of God's kingdom is called "The Presence of the Future."

2 See George Ladd, "Gospel of the Kingdom" (Eerdmans, Grand Rapids, MI, 1990).

Dig Deeper

The heaviest concentrations of Jesus' teaching on God's kingdom are found in the Sermon on the Mount and in a collection of Jesus' parables found in Matthew 13. Let's dig deeper into these teachings.

1.

Read **Matthew 5–7** and **13**. Highlight the words "kingdom" and "heaven."

2.

Scan through these teachings again and answer some questions:

a. What does it mean to enter or experience the kingdom of heaven?

b. What kinds of behaviors are equated with seeking the kingdom?

c. What types of people will find it easier to enter God's kingdom?

d. Who will find it more difficult?

3.

Write down all the things the kingdom is "like." Reflect on the list. What's in the list that surprises you? What's missing that you would have expected?

Discussion

Think about familiar parables we didn't touch on in this session.
Which stories make more sense now that you see Jesus' main teaching as an announcement of God's kingdom?

How are realities of the kingdom true or not true in your life?

How has your experience with Jesus been a taste of heaven and earth uniting?

Notes

Session 10 | Jesus as the Temple

In the beginning was the Word, and the Word was with God, and the Word was God. He was with God in the beginning. Through him all things were made; without him nothing was made that has been made. In him was life, and that life was the light of all mankind. The light shines in the darkness, and the darkness has not overcome it.

There was a man sent from God whose name was John. He came as a witness to testify concerning that light, so that through him all might believe. He himself was not the light; he came only as a witness to the light.

The true light that gives light to everyone was coming into the world. He was in the world, and though the world was made through him, the world did not recognize him. He came to that which was his own, but his own did not receive him. Yet to all who did receive him, to those who believed in his name, he gave the right to become children of God— children born not of natural descent, nor of human decision or a husband's will, but born of God.

The Word became flesh and made his dwelling among us. We have seen his glory, the glory of the one and only Son, who came from the Father, full of grace and truth.

John 1:1–14 (NIV)

When it was almost time for the Jewish Passover, Jesus went up to Jerusalem. In the temple courts he found people selling cattle, sheep and doves, and others sitting at tables exchanging money. So he made a whip out of cords, and drove all from the temple courts, both sheep and cattle; he scattered the coins of the money changers and overturned their tables. To those who sold doves he said, "Get these out of here! Stop turning my Father's house into a market!" His disciples remembered that it is written: "Zeal for your house will consume me."

The Jews then responded to him, "What sign can you show us to prove your authority to do all this?"

Jesus answered them, "Destroy this temple, and I will raise it again in three days."

They replied, "It has taken forty-six years to build this temple, and you are going to raise it in three days?" But the temple he had spoken of was his body. After he was raised from the dead, his disciples recalled what he had said. Then they believed the scripture and the words that Jesus had spoken.

John 2:13–22 (NIV)

Jesus Rages at the Merchants

During the spring holiday of Passover, hundreds of thousands of ancient Israelites flocked to Jerusalem to celebrate the story of their ancestors' exodus from Egypt. One year, around 30 A.D., Jesus and his disciples were among them—and caused a scene witnesses were unlikely to ever forget.

It was common for merchants to sell animals near the temple during Passover. Some Jews traveled from distant villages to visit the temple for the holiday, and they often did not bring animals with them on their journey.

It was also common for money changers to set up shop among the vendors. After all, those visitors from all over the region wanted to buy animals for sacrifice. These businessmen made a hefty profit exchanging their clients' foreign cash for local coins.

There are a handful of passages in later Jewish texts (called the Talmud and the Mekhilta) that preserve a memory of Caiaphas the high priest allowing merchants and money changers into the temple precincts. This is precisely what Jesus seems to be reacting against.

What was new that year was that the high priest had recently decided to relocate all this business from outside the temple walls to inside the sacred courtyard—the latest in a recent series of corrupt decisions on the part of Israel's high priest. This space was supposed to be set aside for worship, repentance, and prayer. Now it was a place for merchants to make serious cash.

And Jesus was having none of this.

Jesus loved the temple, as did all faithful Jews. It was the place where heaven had overlapped with earth, the place God made his presence available to his people. So when Jesus found that it had become a corrupted shell of the beautiful symbol it once was, he overflowed with righteous anger.

There had also been issues with corruption hundreds of years earlier, and many Old Testament passages pointed to the need for its purification, including Zechariah 14:20–21 and Malachi 3:1–4. It seems that these texts were part of Jesus' motivation for his startling actions.

Jesus came in swinging. Armed with a homemade whip, he turned over the tables of the money changers, scattering coins all over the floor of the temple, likely scaring everyone present, including their animals. People must have thought Jesus had gone crazy as he yelled at the merchants, "Stop turning my Father's house into a market!"

Jesus was behaving like one of Israel's ancient prophets, who would often perform outrageous public stunts to generate controversy and draw attention to their message. He was not only staging a protest, he was enacting a symbol. By bringing the sacrificial system to a halt at least for a little while, and declaring it all corrupt, he was declaring God's justice on the temple. This becomes clear by the conversation that follows.

Jesus Responds With a Riddle

The Jewish leaders immediately confronted Jesus, asking what authority he had to waltz in and act like he owned the place. As a challenge to Jesus, the leaders demanded that he perform a sign to prove he was a prophet. Instead, he responded with a riddle:

> *"Destroy this temple, and I will raise it again in three days."*
>
> John 2:19 (NIV)

Huh? What does this have to do with anything? Why is he talking about temples being destroyed? And what is the "three days" referring to?

The people confronting Jesus clearly thought he was talking about the temple building. It had been destroyed before, when the Israelites were exiled to Babylon. A less-impressive version was rebuilt when they returned around 520 B.C. By Jesus' time, a total renovation was decades underway, some 46 years in the making. Everyone knew that rebuilding this kind of magnificent structure in three days was crazy talk.

Nebuchadnezzar besieged Jerusalem and destroyed Solomon's beautiful temple in 587 B.C.

Jesus as a Human Temple

But Jesus wasn't talking about the temple building. He was talking about himself.

Let's be clear: Jesus was calling himself a temple, therefore claiming that God dwelled in him. This was such a strange thing to do that no one in the moment caught on. In John's Gospel, John takes a break in the story to tell readers that even he didn't understand the riddle at the time. God dwelled in temple buildings, in the sky, in all the earth. He didn't dwell in people.

John 2:21–22: "The temple he had spoken of was his body. After he was raised from the dead, his disciples recalled what he had said. Then they believed the scripture and the words that Jesus had spoken."

But there Jesus was, claiming to be the place where God and humanity met together in harmony.

This is how John and the other disciples eventually came to see Jesus as well, and that's why John begins his Gospel with that famous line in 1:14, "The Word became flesh and made his dwelling among us." The Hebrew word translated as "dwelling" is the same word for "tabernacle" in the Old Testament.

Jesus literally and metaphorically tabernacled among us.

In John 1:14, the Greek word for "made his dwelling" is *skenao*, the verb form of the noun *skene*, which means "tent" or "tabernacle."

Jesus constantly did and said things that implied that he was taking over the role of the temple, such as forgiving people of their sins. Normally, Israelites would sacrifice a lamb or goat at the temple as a means of atonement to cover their sins. Then Jesus came along, announcing that people's sins are atoned for simply because he said so.

As if this weren't category-busting enough, Jesus' cryptic riddle was a prediction of his death and resurrection. The Jewish leaders would in fact destroy Jesus, and he would in fact raise his body in three days.

This connects to another claim included in John's Gospel. In John 1:29, John the Baptist sees Jesus and shouts, "Look, the Lamb of God, who takes away the sin of the world!" Jesus was not only the first human temple, but also the ultimate sacrifice.

The "lamb of God" is a rich Old Testament image that either refers to the lambs made as purification offerings for Israel's sins or to the lamb that was slain for the Passover meal.

Jesus did do away with the sacrificial system. Not by turning over tables, but by canceling the need for sacrifice with his own death.

With this riddle, Jesus was saying the only sign that would prove his authority was his voluntary death and miraculous resurrection. The body of the risen Jesus would be the new temple, the fulfillment of the promise spoken of by the ancient prophets.

Geek Out

The Messiah's Zeal for the Temple

Jesus' angry outburst in the temple may seem a bit extreme for modern readers. But his response had an ancient pedigree among Israel's prophets, and this helps us understand what Jesus thought he was doing with that whip.

The temple was considered a royal institution—a place that was built, overseen, and protected by kings. Kings also appointed priests. In ancient Jerusalem, Solomon's temple stood next to the royal palace.

When Solomon's temple fell into disarray, and was eventually destroyed by the Babylonians, Israel's prophets blamed the kings, especially Manasseh, who had introduced the worship of Canaanite idols into the temple precincts. The prophets viewed the destruction and exile as divine justice.

Read Manasseh's story in 2 Kings 21, and the prophetic critique of Manasseh in Jeremiah 15.

After exile, the prophets channeled all of this disappointment with Israel's kings into hope for the future. The prophets believed that one day God would send a new and better king from David's line to rebuild and honor the holiness of the temple. If Israel's present king can't be trusted to protect the temple, then God would send a king someday who would change all that. The Messiah would come and clean house.

In Hebrew, this king was called *hamashiach*, or in English, "the messiah," which translates to "anointed king."

In Zechariah 14:21, the prophet wrote: "And on that day there will no longer be a *Canaanite* in the house of the Lord of Hosts." The word Hebrew word for Canaanite, *kena'aniy*, was also a common term for "merchant" or "trader," and that's more likely what the prophet intended here. Zechariah hoped a new king would come and restore the temple to a place of pure worship, a place where people could truly experience heaven and earth reunited, a place unsullied by greed and economic one-upmanship.

Zechariah lived in the period after the exile and the building of the second temple. The fact that he still hoped for yet another king and temple shows that he did not view the events of his own day as the fulfillment of the ancient prophetic promises.

Jesus knew the Old Testament Scriptures by heart, and there's no doubt the prophets' hope for this future king was on his mind that day in the temple.

He was that future king. And on that day in the temple, he kicked out the merchants, just like the prophets said he would.

Geek Out

Israel vs. The Establishment

Outrage at the temple establishment didn't start or end with Jesus. We know from other historical sources that Jesus was not alone in his disgust for what was happening there. At this time in history, the position of the high priesthood was sold to the highest bidder, and prone to corruption.

One community in particular stands out for their pushback against the temple establishment. A breakaway sect lived in the desert near a place that today is called "Qumran." Here lived a radical Jewish group know for producing the Dead Sea Scrolls. The community's leadership included a number of former priests who had withdrawn to the wilderness to protest the temple's corruption.

The Dead Sea Scrolls were preserved for 2,000 years in clay jars and discovered in 1948.

Not long before Jesus' time, the group's leaders had even sent a letter to the priests in Jerusalem debating the technicalities of how the sacred worship rituals were being performed. (Think Marin Luther's 99 theses, but without a Reformation.) The group was also responsible for crafting a collection of commentary text on Old Testament Scriptures. One of these, which focused on the short book of Habakkuk, called the high priest in Jerusalem, "the wicked priest."

This letter is known today as "4QMMT."

About 30 years after Jesus' death, the Jewish people in and around Jerusalem revolted against the Roman Empire. One of the rebels' first targets was their own high priest, Ananias. They burned his house to the ground and had him executed as an act of revenge, as well as purification. They believed the priesthood had become compromised by negotiating a partnership with the Roman authorities.

Dig Deeper

The Gospel of John presents Jesus as the temple in which heaven and earth overlap as well as the animal sacrifice offered for Israel's sins. This dual presentation of Jesus as both the temple and sacrifice continues throughout the entire New Testament. Let's explore how Paul and Peter incorporate this idea into their teachings.

1.

Read **Colossians 1:19** and **2:9**. Note the different uses of the word "dwell," which is a key temple word associated with God's temple presence.

2.

Read **Colossians 1:20** and **2:13–14**. How does Paul describe Jesus, specifically, the meaning of his death?

3.

Read **Romans 3:24–25, 1 Corinthians 5:7,** and **1 Peter 1:18–19**. Circle the word "blood." How is Jesus described here?

4.

Read **1 Peter 2:4–7** and **Ephesians 2:21–22**. How is Jesus described here?

5.

Take a moment to draw all these texts and their metaphors together: Sacrifices took place in the temple where God's presence dwelled. How does all this help us understand what happened when Jesus died and was raised?

Discussion

Today, we often think of Jesus as "nice," and so we often expect Christians to be nice, too. How does this story challenge that construct?

What does it mean to you that Jesus is God's temple?

What types of things make you so mad that you want to tear something down? How could you use that zeal for furthering the kingdom of heaven?

Notes

Session 11 | Humans as God's Temple

When the day of Pentecost came, they were all together in one place. Suddenly a sound like the blowing of a violent wind came from heaven and filled the whole house where they were sitting. They saw what seemed to be tongues of fire that separated and came to rest on each of them. All of them were filled with the Holy Spirit and began to speak in other languages as the Spirit enabled them.

Acts 2:1–4 (NIV)

Consequently, you are no longer foreigners and strangers, but fellow citizens with God's people and also members of his household, built on the foundation of the apostles and prophets, with Christ Jesus himself as the chief cornerstone. In him the whole building is joined together and rises to become a holy temple in the Lord. And in him you too are being built together to become a dwelling in which God lives by his Spirit.

Ephesians 2:19–22 (NIV)

You also, like living stones, are being built into a spiritual house to be a holy priesthood, offering spiritual sacrifices acceptable to God through Jesus Christ.

1 Peter 2:5 (NIV)

The Spirit Arrives With Fire and Wind

Jesus was not accepted as a legitimate prophet by the leaders of Jerusalem. Eventually, he was arrested and executed with a Roman torture device called a cross.

See John 14:16–17 and 20:21–22.

The night before his execution, Jesus told his disciples that he was leaving, and that he would send them the Holy Spirit as a guide to continue his kingdom mission.

The Spirit arrived on the day of Pentecost, which was a Jewish festival celebrating the end of the harvest. For more about Pentecost, check out Exodus 34:22 and Deuteronomy 16:10.

After his resurrection, Jesus breathed that Spirit onto his circle of 12 disciples. Then, in Acts, we see the Holy Spirit coming to all of Jesus' followers. They were together in a house when they heard the sound of violent wind and saw what appeared to be tongues of fire descending on each of their heads.

Wind? Tongues of fire? What is going on here?

Wind and Fire Symbolize Presence

For the tabernacle, see Exodus 40:34–35. For the temple, see 1 Kings 20:18–21.

In the Old Testament, when God first came to dwell in the tabernacle, his presence appeared in the form of wind and fire settling over the Holy of Holies. The same thing happened at the dedication of Solomon's temple.

For the burning bush, see Exodus 3. For the Mt. Sinai story, see Exodus 20:18–21.

God's arrival at his holy houses wasn't the only time his presence appeared as flames. Moses met God in a burning bush and later received the Ten Commandments in a fire storm atop Mt. Sinai.

So, when Luke says tongues of fire descended onto Jesus' followers, he couldn't be more clear: God's presence was arriving and settling into a new temple. But this time, that temple was not a tent or an opulent building. It was the body of Jesus' followers—individually and collectively. They became mini-temples in which God's holy presence dwelled.

Major Implications

We quickly learn in the New Testament that being little temples had major implications for early Christians.

For instance, the Apostle Paul warned followers of Jesus in Corinth not to let their pride divide them. Why? Because he considered it a corruption of God's new temple. He wrote: "Don't you know that you all are God's temple and that God's Spirit dwells in your midst? If anyone destroys God's temple, God will destroy that person; for God's temple is sacred, and you all together are that temple."

This challenge from Paul to the Corinthians is found in 1 Corinthians 3:16–17. You can't tell in English, but in Greek all the words for "you" are plural, referring to all the Corinthians collectively.

That's intense. Apparently being the sacred temple of God came with serious communal responsibility.

Paul also used mini-temple status as the foundation for calling new believers to change their behavior and view their bodies differently. One group of men in the Corinth church had continued their pre-conversion habit of eating ritual meals in the local pagan temple and sleeping with the prostitutes who worked there. Paul called them out, saying, "Do you not know that your bodies are temples of the Holy Spirit, who is in you, whom you have received from God? You are not your own; you were bought at a price. Therefore honor God with your bodies."

This challenge from Paul is found in 1 Corinthians 6:12–20.

This reality, being God's temple, is foundational to the entire New Testament and to the church's identity as "Jesus' body." The early Christians saw themselves as the place where heaven and earth overlapped.

Being God's temple also meant a shift in vocation. As mini-temples, furthering the kingdom became top priority for the early Christians. They were told to go out to all the nations to share the good news that Jesus is the risen king of the world, spreading God's presence as they went. Jesus inaugurated the kingdom of heaven, and his disciples were tasked with multiplying and subduing the earth with it. This was a reboot of the blessing given to Adam and Eve to multiply and subdue the earth. It was a fulfillment of God's promise to bless all the nations through the Israelites.

It was also the beginning of God's fulfillment of the prophets' dreams that a future anointed king, or "messiah," would build a new temple and return the Promised Land to God's people—but it didn't look quite like they expected. Instead of a temple building, God raised a temple through a body of believers. And instead of returning Jerusalem to the Israelites, he began restoring all of creation to a renewed humanity, for the whole earth is his Promised Land.

The Holy Spirit Purifies

Now, remember, entering God's temple required ritual cleansing—ever since God came to dwell in the tabernacle after rescuing the Israelites from Egypt. It had been essential to keep symbols of death and decay out of the temple.

For purity laws, check out Leviticus 12–15.

If Christians are God's new temple, do they have to uphold the same purity laws?

Well, no and yes. Followers of Jesus are not bound to any one city, much less ancient Jerusalem with its temple. So, "no," we don't have to carry out the sacrificial rituals and the holiness rites specific to the ancient Israelite culture.

But let us quickly follow that up with a "yes"; followers of Jesus do have a serious responsibility to maintain purity as mini-temples. The divine presence of Jesus is with his people through the Holy Spirit, and this reality should reshape every aspect of our lives and our behavior. It should bring our understanding of good and evil back into line with God's wisdom. In our speech, our bodies, and in all of our relationships.

Being God's temple is a serious task. The temple was a symbolic microcosm of heaven on earth, and death has no place in that space. It is dedicated and set apart for life and beauty and all that is good.

Peter's use of temple imagery to describe Jesus' followers can be found in 1 Peter 2:1–11.

This is why Peter surrounds his discussion of the church as the new temple with challenges to a new way of life: "Rid yourselves of all malice and all deceit, hypocrisy, envy, and slander of every kind." And then later, "Abstain from sinful desires, which wage war against your soul."

The church is the place where God's domain is invading humans' domain, right here in the midst of the old creation. And even more personally, right there inside your own body. The church is the new humanity. Destructive behaviors that ruin people and healthy relationships have no place here. The new temple is set apart for humans to rediscover their true identity as images of God. It's the place where people learn they are beloved children who have been liberated to know the holy God and his love for them. It's a space of healing and hope, for everyone.

Geek Out

The Spirit and the Temple

There is a remarkably close connection between the Holy Spirit and God's temples in the Bible, and it goes well beyond the wind and fire symbols we explored earlier in this session.

On page one of the Bible, the author of Genesis introduces the Spirit as the key agent through whom God created the universe as his temple, saying the Spirit of God was hovering over the chaos. From the very beginning, the Spirit was closely linked to the creation of temples.

See Genesis 1:2.

"Spirit" was also how the Old Testament authors talked about the personal, invisible, and powerful presence of the Creator God at work within the world. In Hebrew, the word for "Spirit" is spelled *ruakh*, and refers to "wind" or "breath." This word is repeatedly used by biblical authors to identify God's energetic presence in the world long before Jesus came on the scene.

A great example of this comes from Exodus, when a man named Bezalel was commissioned by God as the lead designer of the tabernacle. We're told he was "filled with the Spirit of God, with wisdom and understanding." Similar to Genesis 1, God's Spirit was at work in the world to create a temple, but this time through an empowered human agent designing a mobile tent.

Read about Bezalel and his Spirit empowerment in Exodus 31:1–11.

Later in Israel's story, after the Jerusalem temple had been destroyed, God's Spirit played a key role in the future hope of the prophets. When Ezekiel imagined a new temple and a new, obedient Israel, he knew that both would have to be the work of God's Spirit. In Ezekiel 36, we find the promise that God's creative presence would one day come to live inside his own people, just as it once lived inside the tabernacle and the temple. Ezekiel believed God's Spirit would recreate the hearts of his people so that they could truly love and obey him.

| Geek Out

The Spirit and the Temple (cont.)

He wrote:

> *I will give you a new heart and put a new spirit in you; I will remove from you your heart of stone and give you a heart of flesh. And I will put my Spirit inside you and move you to follow my decrees and be careful to keep my laws…you will be my people, and I will be your God.*
>
> Ezekiel 36:26–28 (NIV)

Ezekiel's famous vision about the valley of dry bones draws most of its language and imagery from the depiction of humanity's creation in Genesis 1:26–28 and 2:7.

After this remarkable promise, we find in Ezekiel 37 a symbolic vision that explores this Spirit-filled humanity. Ezekiel sees a replay of Genesis 2, as God's Spirit comes to enliven human bodies. But instead of bringing to life a newly formed human as he did in the garden, God's Spirit fills a valley of dead bodies, remaking them as new humans. Then, as the culmination of God's rescue mission, Ezekiel's vision includes a promise from God to make an "everlasting covenant" with the recreated people and to "put [his] sanctuary among them forever."

Old Testament passages like these from Ezekiel were foundational for the statements of Jesus, Peter, and Paul establishing the new covenant people of God as the new temple.

Geek Out

An Enlightened Sect

The concept of a human as a temple was not common in the Jewish culture of Jesus' day. But he wasn't the only person who had such an idea.

Remember that sect that lived in the desert, the ones who produced the Dead Sea Scrolls and wrote commentaries on Old Testament Scripture? They too shared Jesus' anger at the corruption of the temple and railed against its priesthood.

They reflected on the same prophetic text that inspired Jesus, and so they too discerned that the new temple promised by the Old Testament prophets would not necessarily be a building, but could be a "sanctuary of humans."

In a document scholars call "4QFlorilegium," this sect of strictly observant Israelites expounds on this idea, writing that this future "sanctuary of humans" would "offer sacrifices before God, namely obedience to the Torah." They believed that their small, obedient community was, in fact, the new temple, not the corrupted monstrosity standing in Jerusalem. Their hope was for a future king to drive corruption out of Jerusalem and invite their community to become Israel's new temple leaders.

All of the Dead Sea Scrolls are categorized in the following way:

- A number indicating in which of the 11 caves the scroll was found.
- An abbreviation of the location. For instance, "Q" stands for "Qumran."
- A summary title of the scroll's contents, often in Latin. For instance, "florilegium" is a Latin term for a compilation of excerpts.

Thus, "4QFlorilegium" means "the collection of excerpts found in cave number four at Qumran."

The Old Testament texts explored in the scroll are 2 Samuel 7:10-14, Exodus 15:17-18, and Amos 9:11.

This is fascinating because it shows that Jesus was not alone in claiming that the new temple promised by the prophets was not a new building, but a new community led by an anointed king, or "messiah."

We know that this group was still around in Jesus' time. They were driven from the desert about 30 years after his death—around the same time as the Jewish revolt in Jerusalem. But what we don't know is if any members of this sect became followers of Jesus. They had long hoped to be the new human temple, but whether any of them realized this dream remains a fascinating question that is now lost to history.

Dig Deeper

Peter thought it was essential that new believers understand their role, individually and collectively, as the new temple of God. Let's dig into the language he used to teach this concept to Jesus' followers.

1.

Read **1 Peter 2:4–10**, and underline all the words associated with "house," "temple," and "stone." Why is Peter calling humans "stones"?

2.

Peter quotes from **Isaiah 8:14, 28:16,** and **Psalm 118:22**. Read each verse and consider why Peter quoted from these texts. What do they all have in common?

3.

Read all of **1 Peter 2:4–10** again, this time underlining all the words related to "priests," "sacrifice," and "praise." Why is Peter emphasizing the priesthood?

Discussion

How do you experience the Holy Spirit purifying you on a daily basis?

**What does it mean that we are collectively God's temple?
How does this change the way you think about the church, both locally and globally?**

Paul challenged early Christians to behave in a way that honored their inner temple. What things in your life are not consistent with the sacred task of being God's temple?

Notes

Session 12 | The New Heavens and The New Earth

Jesus said to them, "Truly I tell you, at the renewal of all things, when the Son of Man sits on his glorious throne, you who have followed me will also sit on twelve thrones, judging the twelve tribes of Israel. And everyone who has left houses or brothers or sisters or father or mother or wife[s] or children or fields for my sake will receive a hundred times as much and will inherit eternal life. But many who are first will be last, and many who are last will be first.

Matthew 19:28–30 (NIV)

I consider that the sufferings of this present time are not worth comparing with the glory about to be revealed to us. For the creation waits with eager longing for the revealing of the children of God; for the creation was subjected to futility, not of its own will but by the will of the one who subjected it, in hope that the creation itself will be set free from its bondage to decay and will obtain the freedom of the glory of the children of God. We know that the whole creation has been groaning in labor pains until now…

Romans 8:18–22 (NRSV)

Then I saw a new heaven and a new earth; for the first heaven and the first earth had passed away, and the sea was no more… And the One seated on the throne said: "See, I am making all things new"… And in the spirit he carried me away to a great, high mountain and showed me the holy city Jerusalem coming down out of heaven from God. It has the glory of God and a radiance like a very rare jewel, like jasper, clear as crystal… I saw no temple in the city, for its temple is the Lord God the Almighty and the Lamb.

Revelation 21 (NRSV)

The Apostles Hoped for A New Creation

Earlier in this workbook, we explored the Old Testament prophetic hope for the renewal of all creation—a time when God's domain and humans' domain would fully reunite. Remember, the prophets used imaginative language to describe this new creation, saying milk would stream down hills, and wild animals would play with babies.

Jesus' apostles shared this simple hope. They believed Jesus had started that recreation process and raised a new temple, but it was clear that not all of creation had been renewed.

See Romans 8:21.

When Paul reflected on this future hope, he said the world would one day be "liberated from its bondage to decay"—a glorious freedom we're still waiting for today.

At this present moment, the earth is cut off from the full life of heaven. To use a biblical metaphor, it groans like a woman in childbirth. But the new creation is here, taking form even when we can't see it. We do sense hints of it now and then, though, just like we might make out an elbow or foot poking from within a pregnant woman's belly. One day it will be pushed forth into life, like a new baby emerging from the womb.

All New Things or All Things New?

In the last book of the Bible, the Revelation, we witness John's symbolic vision of that great rebirth. He saw a new heaven and earth—a clear reference to the very beginning of the biblical narrative.

In this vision, John presents us with a paradox. As soon as he finishes saying, "I saw a new heaven and earth" and that the first creation has "passed away," John says he heard God announce: "Behold, I am making all things new."

For this important climactic vision, see Revelation 21:1–5.

So, is God making all things new, or is he making all new things?

To answer that question, we have to go back to the source of John's hope: the resurrected Jesus. The risen Jesus was physical, not a ghost. He ate food and drank wine and talked with his followers about the kingdom of God over the course of a few weeks. He had scars on his hands and feet. There was no mistake. They were touching and talking with the same Jesus they followed up in the hills of Galilee.

The accounts of Jesus' resurrection appearances to the disciples are found in Matthew 28, Mark 16, Luke 24, and John 20-21.

But the resurrected Jesus was also different. Really different. Some of the disciples didn't even recognize him at first glance. And while Jesus' body was physical, it was physical in a way that was clearly different from ours. He inexplicably appeared and disappeared from rooms, baffling the disciples. There were no categories that prepared them for this moment, so all they could do is tell the odd stories we find in the New Testament.

In John 20:19, the risen Jesus appeared suddenly in a room with a locked door. See Luke 24:31 and 24:36 for similar surprises.

This paradox of "the same Jesus and also a different Jesus" is precisely what John was trying to communicate about the "new heavens and earth" in the book of Revelation. He was convinced that the future of the universe walked out of the tomb on Easter morning, simultaneously the same and different. What was true of the risen Jesus is what will be true for all creation when heaven and earth completely reunite.

Symbols of a New Creation

This is why John used apocalyptic symbols and metaphors to describe this event, just like the Old Testament prophets used poetry. He wasn't transcribing a video-perfect version of what was to come. Rather, he was attempting to express an unexplainable conviction. Sometimes, only metaphors and symbols will suffice.

John's vision about the new creation is in Revelation 21:1–5.

John first described the new creation as a marriage of heaven and earth. Heaven is represented as both a city and a bride, coming down out of God's heavenly domain and landing on earth, much like the staircase Jacob saw in his dream. John called the city-bride a "new Jerusalem." It was so marvelous that he could only describe it in terms of brilliant stones.

The precious stones John lists to describe the new Jerusalem are taken from the list of jewels that decorated the high priest's breastplate in Exodus 28:15–21.

Jerusalem itself was a powerful symbol for John. It was the first and only city where God resided in a permanent holy house, the first city where kings worshiped the true Creator. At the heart of the Israelites' Promised Land, Jerusalem represented the ultimate Promised Land: all of restored creation.

He depicts the reunion of heaven and earth as the descent of a new Jerusalem. Unlike the old Jerusalem that was corrupted and dishonored by most of Israel's kings, the new Jerusalem would be ruled by a divine king. This new city would be built by God, not by human hands.

John adopted most of his new temple and new Jerusalem imagery from the prophets Isaiah (see Isaiah 2, 11, 60–62) and Ezekiel (see Ezekiel 40–48).

John also employed the Garden of Eden as an image to describe the renewed creation. He saw the tree of life there, accessible to all and eternally yielding fruit. It could do this because its roots had access to the eternal river of life, which can dispense nourishment to all the new creation because it flows from the presence of God himself.

But in John's account of a garden, humanity wasn't represented by a couple. John describes seeing all the nations there, working to cultivate the garden as Adam and Eve did in Genesis. For John, the fulfillment of God's purpose through Jesus would result in the restoration of humans to their place as co-rulers of God's world, ready to work with God to take creation into uncharted territory.

The end of the biblical story is really a new beginning.

Unanswered Questions

John's visions leave most of our questions about the new creation unanswered—and that's not a bad thing. John's goal wasn't to satisfy our curiosity about the new world, but to instill confidence that the creation would be reborn just as Jesus was resurrected from the dead.

This is the hope of the story of the Bible: God's domain and our domain will one day completely unite. All things will be made new. Death will be replaced with life. The whole earth will be a recreation of the garden, and the glory of the temple will fill the whole earth. Every nation will be blessed through the power of the resurrected Jesus, and God's own personal presence will permeate every square inch of the new creation.

Geek Out

Literally Metaphorical

John was a master of the Hebrew Scriptures, and his vision of the new creation is a kaleidoscope of images drawn from the biblical poets and prophets. His goal was to create a visual collage of Old Testament metaphors that forces us to reckon with the meaning of these images.

A great example is John's physical descriptions of the new Jerusalem in Revelation 21:15–21. He says the heavenly city has four sides, each with three gates, corresponding to the 12 tribes of Israel. Then he mentions 12 huge foundation stones, which correspond to the 12 apostles. After this, John says the heavenly city is a perfect cube, each side being 12,000 stadia, or 1,400 miles. Then we're told that the walls were 144 cubits high, or about 200 feet.

For the 12 gates of Ezekiel's vision, see Ezekiel 48:31–34.

For Jesus' selection of 12 disciples, see Matthew 10:1–4 and 19:28.

This sounds like a structure that defies mathematics, and some people leave it at that. But John wasn't trying to document a blueprint. He was using two distinct Old Testament references to craft a deeper meaning. Let's break this down:

- The image of a city on a high hill with 12 gates corresponding to the 12 tribes of Israel is adapted from Ezekiel's vision of the new Jerusalem in Ezekiel 40.
- The concept of a cube is derived from 1 Kings 6:19–20, which specifies that the Holy of Holies in Solomon's temple was cubic in shape.

The cuboid Holy of Holies (20 x 20 x 20 cubits) took up one third of the entire temple space. The outer holy place made up the other two thirds.

The results of combining these references only make sense on a symbolic level. If you try to draw it, the numbers just don't work. But John's goal was to communicate that Ezekiel's idea of a new Jerusalem would actually be one giant temple with the same qualities as the Holy of Holies in Solomon's temple.

Still confused? It means there will be no need for a physical temple or Holy of Holies in the new creation because the fullness of God's presence will be everywhere. All of the new creation will be God's Holy of Holies.

| Geek Out

Do We Go to Heaven When We Die?

The phrase "go *up* to heaven" is found in the Bible, but it doesn't relate to afterlife. Rather, it's used to describe something that is impossible for humans to find. Even if humans could go up into the skies (which, in biblical times, was impossible), you couldn't find what you're looking for. (For examples, see Deuteronomy 30:12 or Proverbs 30:4.)

We've established that the main focus of the biblical story is the union, split and future reunion of God's domain and our domain. We know heaven and earth aren't simply separate living quarters, but they are representations of spaces where God rules and defines good and evil and where humans have staked out their own realm and define good and evil for themselves.

But, so far, our dive into this story hasn't addressed one of our most common and pressing questions: What happens after we die? Don't followers of Jesus "go to heaven?" Isn't going to heaven one of the main things a Christian should hope for?

Get ready for the answer.

There is not even one passage in the Bible that talks about "going to heaven" after you die. The phrase "go to heaven" doesn't appear anywhere in the Old or New Testaments in relation to death. Not once.

This doesn't mean the Bible has nothing to say about what happens to God's people after they die. It just means that "going to heaven" isn't the way biblical authors thought about it. Let's look at the New Testament passages that speak to what Jesus' followers will experience after they die. They all use the same phrase: Our hope is about being "with Jesus."

LUKE 23:42–43
Jesus spoke to the repentant criminal being crucified next to him, saying, "Today you'll be *with me* in paradise."

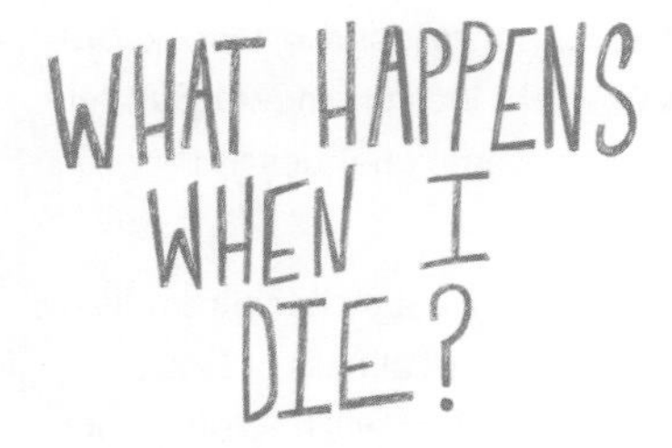

PHILIPPIANS 1:21–24
Paul discussed his possible execution in a Roman prison, and he said death wouldn't be so bad. It would make the Philippians sad, but he would get to be "*with Christ*."

2 CORINTHIANS 5:6–9
Paul talked about the true hope that drives Christian faithfulness, even in the face of death. The result of death, he said, was being "*with the Lord*."

Geek Out

Both Jesus and Paul believed that not even death could separate people from God's love, and that Jesus' followers would be with him after death.

See Philippians 3:20–21, Romans 6:4–6 and 1 Corinthians 15:20–28.

However, Paul does not envision this disembodied mode of existence as permanent, or even desirable. In 2 Corinthians 5:2 (NIV), Paul wrote that in this world "we groan, longing to be clothed with our *heavenly dwelling*." He's referring here to a resurrected body believers will inherit when they are finally made like Jesus. For Paul, the end goal is not disembodied bliss in heaven, but rather a restored physical existence, which is a gift from heaven.

But what about the interim period, when our mortal bodies rot in the ground?

For uses of "falling asleep," see Acts 7:60, 1 Thessalonians 4:13, John 11:11, 2 Peter 3:4, and 1 Corinthians 15:20.

Paul describes this interim experience as "falling asleep." And he wasn't alone in using sleep as a metaphor for death. It was common in Jewish culture. The phrase "lay down with my ancestors" was a common Old Testament way to describe death. The prophets described death as a form of sleep and the hope of future resurrection as "waking up."

Remember that these are poetic metaphors, so we shouldn't analyze them for precise information about what we will experience after we die. Some people believe we'll essentially be unconscious until the new creation is fully realized. Others expect to be with Jesus right away.

Whichever view you hold, the takeaway is clear: Death is not the end for followers of Jesus. Just as he went through death and came out the other side in a transformed physical existence, so also his people can hope for the same. Our ultimate hope is to inhabit reborn creation with the one who died was reborn on our behalf.

Dig Deeper

We've learned a lot in these 12 sessions, and that new information is likely to reshape the way you read Scripture. Let's revisit the Bible's bookends:

1.

Read **Genesis 1–2**, which describes the original heavens and earth. Then, read **Revelation 21–22**, which describes the reborn heavens and earth.
Write down every image that appears in both accounts. What's the same?
What's different?

2.

Do it again. You'll notice new things. We promise. And as you do, you'll be invited into the brilliance of John's mind as he crafted his vision of the renewed creation.

Discussion

What questions do you have about what the new creation will be like?

Does this future reality seem comforting? Strange? Exhilarating? Explain.

How would you change if your hope was in the future reunification of heaven and earth?

Notes

Conclusion

The Bible is a unified story that leads us to Jesus—the one in whom heaven and earth are being reunited. Our hope of seeing God's domain and our domain fully rejoined is what drives us to follow Jesus and pray that more of heaven invades more of earth, and more of us.

the UNION of HEAVEN & EARTH

IS WHAT THE

Story

of the

BIBLE

IS

ALL

ABOUT

Acknowledgments

Co-writing this workbook was a fun process of discovery for both us. We launched The Bible Project with the Heaven and Earth video, and we always felt that these ideas were worth exploring in greater depth. Jon cranked out the first draft; then Tim made it too long and wordy; then Jon made it concise again, and so on! We're grateful for the wise editing skills of Melissa Binder who helped us bring coherence to the entire workbook. The illustrations were created by the talented Robert Perez, Mac Cooper and Sheila Laufer, and the layout design comes from the creative mind of Xela Gold. Thanks to Miriam Chesbro for juggling all the balls necessary to keep the project moving forward, and thank you Whitney Woollard for your love of copy editing and proper English grammar!

Exploring the relationship between heaven and earth in the Bible has been a transformative experience for both of us. We hope that your imagination and your heart are captured by this amazing story. May you think bigger and better thoughts about how you could join Jesus in his mission to reunite heaven and earth.

Tim Mackie & Jon Collins

Thank you for using this workbook! We hope it has aided you in seeing how the theme of Heaven and Earth weaves through Scripture and ties the story of the Bible together.

The Bible Project is crowdfunded non-profit devoted to explaining the Bible as a unified story that leads to Jesus. We create short films that are free to watch and download as well as supplemental material (like this workbook) that expands on our videos. This workbook is free to download in PDF form from our website. From there you can also join the growing number of people who support this endeavor.

The Bible Project is an ecumenical project serving all Christian traditions. We are located in Portland, Oregon. Please say hi!

twitter.com/joinbibleproj

facebook.com/thebibleproject

instagram.com/thebibleproject/

thebibleproject.com